ARAMAIC WORD STUDY

EXPLORING THE LANGUAGE OF THE NEW TESTAMENT

Chaim Bentorah

Copyright © 2021 Chaim Bentorah Ministries All rights reserved.

No part of this publication may be reproduced, stored, or transmitted in any form or by any means, including written, copied, or electronically, without prior written permission from the author or his agents. The only exception is brief quotations in printed reviews. Short excerpts may be used with the publisher's or author's expressed written permission.

All Scripture quotations, unless otherwise noted, are from the King James Version of the Bible.

A Hebrew Teacher Looks At Stargates, Time Travel, and Alternate Universes

Cover and Interior Page design by True Potential, Inc.

ISBN: (Paperback): 9781953247513

ISBN: (e-book): 9781953247520

LCCN: 2021947995

True Potential, Inc.

PO Box 904, Travelers Rest, SC 29690

www.truepotentialmedia.com

Produced and Printed in the United States of America.

CONTENTS

INTRODUCTION	7
1. TAKE UP SNAKES	13
2. BROKEN – QATSA'	16
3. OUTER DARKNESS – CHOSHUKA BARI	19
4. WEAKNESS - KORAH	22
5. LISTEN TO MY HEART, THIS IS MY DESTINY	24
6. UNDIVORCED – SHEVAQ	27
7. WOUNDED LOVE – CHAV	30
8. LOVING SERVICE – 'AVAD	34
9. THE BROKEN LETTER HEI	37
10. THE WEDDING DANCE – CHADOTHA	40
11. MANSIONS – 'ONA	43
12. DIPLOMACY – SHU'ABDA	46
13. WHILE REJOICING - KAD CHADA'	49
14. BE OPEN - ETHPATHACH	51
15. DIVINE LOVE – RAV CHESSED	54
16. RICH AND POOR – 'ATAR MASAK	57
17. TONGUES OF FIRE LASHANA NORA'	60
18. THE (THIRD) TEMPLE - BEIT HAMIQADASH	63
19. O YOU OF LITTLE FAITH - 'ANATHON ZE'ORI HIMANUTHA	66
20. APPLAUSE – SEPHAQ	69
21. EMBRACE OF SUFFERING – CHASHA	73

22. THE THRONE OF GRACE – KURSIA TIVOTA	75
23. MERCY SEAT – CHUSAVA'	78
24. LOVE GIFT – MOHABATA	81
25. VERY NEARLY – BAQALIL	84
26. RICH IN LOVE – DA'ATIR BARACHAMUHI	87
27. ARMOR THAT SHINES – ZINA	90
28. LAY IT ALL OUT – PERASH	92
29. HIGH PRIEST – RABKUMRA'	95
30. MOCKED – BAZACH	98
31. TRANSFORMATION – NSIONA	101
32. FALL IN LOVE WITH GOD – 'EVED	104
33. ANGELS UNAWARE - LO RAGASH MALAKA	107
34. GROWING CORN – QOM	111
35. LAWYERS – SAPHRA	114
36. LIVING WATERS – MIA CHI	117
37. CAST OUT – NEPHAQ	120
38. PREACHING IN THE WILDERNESS	122
39. VIPERS –'AKIDNA'	125
40. MALEFACTOR – 'AVAD BISHA	127
41. THE COCK CROWS – QARA' TARANAGALA'	129
42. AND YOU ARE IN ME - 'ANATHON BI	133
43. LITTLE CHILD – TELA'	136
44. BONDSERVANTS – 'AVADA	139
45. IT IS FINISHED – MASHELEM	141
46. MY TEACHER – RABBONI	144
47. NO PLACE FOR THEM - LITH DOKA	147
48. EATING AND DRINKING – 'ECHOL VASHATA'	150
49. SON OF MAN - BREH DENASHA	153
50. LITTLE TWIGS - CHAV	156

51. BIND AND LOOSEN   159
52. LET YOUR LIGHT SHINE – NANOOHAR NOOHARKVA   162
53. COLD WATER – GAR   165
54. WHEN YOU PRAY – TSALU 'ANATIN   167
55. AIR KISS – SEGAD   170
56. FAIL - NAPHAL   173
57. ASKING IN THE FLESH   177
58. RECEIVE – QAVAL   180
59. ADOPTION – 'IMUTS   183
60. TAKE NO THOUGHT – YITSEPH   186
61. HOSANNA – HOSHI'AH   189
62. GEHENNA   192
63. WASHING HANDS – SHUG 'AIDA   195
64. WOMAN – 'ANATH   197
65. TRUTH   200
66. GOOD (SHEPHERD)   203
67. REBUKE – KA'A   205
68. THE WAY   209
69. WHERE IS THY STING   211
70. DEMON/MENTAL ILLNESS - DEWANA   214
71. SIMULATED WORSHIP   217
72. BELIEVE – HAYMAN   220
73. JOYFUL MESSAGE – TSEVA   223
74. LET THIS CUP PASS FROM ME   226
75. MERCY - YOD   229

ACKNOWLEDGEMENTS

Thank you to my long-time study and ministry partner Laura Bertone. Your insight and contribution is invaluable.

Thank you to our All-Access Hebrew Word Study Members. You have been an inspiration to this dusty old ancient languages professor.

"As iron sharpens iron, So a man sharpens the countenance of his friend."
Proverbs 27:17

INTRODUCTION

It is important that the reader understands some very real problems with attempting to translate the New Testament from the Aramaic. First, most biblical scholars believe that the language Jesus and his disciples, as well as the Apostle Paul, spoke was an Old Galilean Aramaic or Jewish Palestinian Aramaic, which is a dialect of the Western Aramaic known as a Northern dialect. There are many modern Eastern Neo-Aramaic dialects, but no known Western dialect exists today. It is believed to be a dead language, although, in recent years, three villages in Syria, it was discovered, still speak a dialect known as the Ma'lula dialect, which is believed to be a descendent of the Western dialect and possibly closely related to the Old Galilean. This dialect is being studied, and grammars have been written and discarded. There is just no real certainty other than a few grammatical points as to whether we have a comprehensive knowledge of the language that Jesus spoke.

When Mel Gibson produced his movie *The Passion of the Christ*, he trained his actors to speak the Old Galilean. However, there were many gaps filled in with other known dialects of Aramaic and Arabic, and their language only carried traces of the Old Galilean. To make matters even more difficult, there are no known New Testament documents written in the Old Galilean.

After the destruction of the Temple in 70 AD, there was a migration of Jewish scholars from Judea to Galilee who wrote the Jerusalem Talmud and the Rabbahs in a Northern dialect of Aramaic, a descendent of the Old Galilean that Jesus and His disciples spoke. This dialect, however, was lost during the Byzantine period, and with the rise of the Patriarchal Caliphate, the Northern dialect was replaced by the Arabic language around the seventh century AD. All the manuscripts that were written in the Northern dialect were turned over to Eastern Aramaic-speaking scribes who discovered what they believed were many errors as they recopied the manuscripts over the next thousand years. They "corrected these errors" with an Eastern dialect, though. Only recently have there been discoveries of manuscripts in the original Northern dialect, which showed the original works that were uncorrected by the Eastern scribes and found to really have been correct in the first place as these so-called errors were just a peculiarity of the original language.

The point is that we have no real documents of the original Old Galilean dialect that Jesus spoke. The belief that the Christian New Testament was originally written in Aramaic is only a theory. It is believed that when it was written, a scribe would have translated the words of Jesus and the disciples directly into Greek. However, there is the belief that these words were written as Jesus and the disciples dictated them in the Old Galilean Aramaic, which worked its way into the Syriac language, which is a close cousin of the Northern Dialect and became what is known today as the Peshitta New Testament.

The Assyrian Church of the East, also known as the Nestorian Church, traditionally considers the Syriac version of the New Testament, the Peshitta, to be the original New Testament and the Aramaic to be its original language. However, this is not supported by the majority of scholars, and in fact, it is believed that the Peshitta was translated from the Greek.

However, even in the nineteenth century Ezra Stiles, the President of Yale, was quoted as saying that the Syriac was the daughter voice of the Hebrew during the Apostolic age and that the Syriac Testament would be of high authority if not the same authority of the Greek. This suggests the Syriac was the closest known language to the Northern dialect and that the Syriac version of the New Testament, aka the Peshitta, may have been the language that the New Testament was written in and later translated into Greek.

The Patriarch of the Eastern Catholic church, Shimun XXI Eshai, declared in 1957 that the originality of the Peshitta text was received by the Eastern Church from the hands of the Apostles themselves in the Aramaic original and that the Peshitta is the text of the Church of the East which has come down from the biblical times without change or revision.

There is even the view by many historical critics that the Greek New Testament may have had Aramaic source texts which no longer exist. It is argued by the Eastern church that there is no evidence that any attempt was made to collect all the Greek manuscripts into one code or canon until after the Second or Third Century, but it is certain that the Syrian Churches had their canon long before this collection was made, traditionally believed to be between the years 55-60 and was done by the Apostle Jude. This canon consisted of all the books of the New Testament except the book of Revelation, II Peter, II John, III John, and Jude and was written in the Syriac before the Greek canon was ever compiled.

However, let's be fair that only a tiny minority of recent scholars are backers of the Peshitta theory, and the overwhelming majority of scholars consider the Peshitta New Testament to be a translation from the Greek original.

So why am I writing a book using the Aramaic or Peshitta as a source? We must keep in mind that all translations of ancient texts are speculative in some manner. This is not to say they are not inspired; it is to just affirm that our translators and historians are not inspired. It behooves us to seek out whatever sources are available to us from the Greek and Aramaic to allow the Holy Spirit to guide us into an understanding of how the original text really read. Even if we had the original manuscripts, would we be able to really understand all the nuances and colloquial expressions that were prevalent in that day? Expressions such as Son of God and Son of Man need a first-century understanding. Even Nicodemus did not understand what Jesus meant by "you must be born again." When Jesus and his disciples journeyed to the southern portion of Israel, their accents and use of idioms and colloquial expressions were quite pronounced. Nicodemus had a problem when Jesus said: *mitheelidh min dresh* (born again). The Southern dialect, which Nicodemus spoke, would have taken this literally as a physical birth. However, the Northern dialect would have expressed more of a broader range of meaning to include a spiritual rebirth. Ultimately, the Holy Spirit is our guide and teacher as we study the Word of God.

My most intense study has been in Classical Hebrew and Mishnaic Aramaic, aka Tannaitic Hebrew or Early Rabbinic Hebrew, used in the Talmud, Mishnah, and some of the Dead Sea Scrolls. However, I have studied the Syriac and its relationship to the Mishnaic Aramaic, and I have made comparative studies of many Syriac words found in the Peshitta to the Mishnaic

Aramaic and Classical Hebrew. I used many resources, including the Dictionary of Targumim, Talmud and Midrashic Literature by Marcus Jastrow (1926), the Davidson Analytical Hebrew and Chaldee Lexicon by Davidson, the Brown Drivers Biggs Lexicon and the linguistical studies of Rabbi Samson Hirsch, as well as many other Jewish sources.

For this book, I used the Greek as my primary guide and the Peshitta as a source to examine the depths of a particular word. For instance, in the story of the woman at the well in John 4, where Jesus asks the woman to bring her husband to Him. The Greek word used for husband is *aner*, which is the word for a male and a husband. However, in the Mishnaic Aramaic as well as the Hebrew, there are two words used for a husband, one is *ba'li*, and the other is an *ishah*. The *ba'li* is a master and/or abusive husband, and the *ishah* is a loving husband, one who sees himself as equal to his wife and not a ruler, master, or owner of his wife. We see the difference in the Hebrew in Hosea 2, where God desires to be called an *ishah*, a beloved husband, and not a *ba'li*, a master, or an abusive husband. Thus, Jesus was asking the woman to bring her abusive husband, and she said she had no abusive husband, to which Jesus said that she spoke the truth, for she had five abusive husbands and the one she was living with was not an abusive husband. As women in that Samaritan culture could not live alone and had to be married, it is the assumption that her present husband was an *ishah*, or a loving husband, who considered her an equal partner in their relationship.

Thus, I reach a conclusion by using Greek, Hebrew, and Aramaic to develop a theory. To be sure, I am not saying that my conclusions are to be taken as dogma and all other sources are wrong. I am only offering to my reader an opportunity to expand their thoughts and maybe reach a deeper understanding of a particular word used in our English Bible. To build in you the same desire that this dusty old biblical language teacher has of reaching a deeper understanding of God's Word through the guidance of the Holy Spirit. I do admit to being speculative in many of my conclusions and ask the reader to keep this in mind as they read this book. However, my speculations are based upon my biased personal experience with a God that I believe with all my heart loves me and that I love in return and hold dear as life itself.

It would do well for orthodox Christians, those who embrace the Word of God as truly inspired and God-breathed, to follow the ongoing research and latest discoveries from archeology and the Dead Sea Scrolls. Many scholars do this research for academic reasons, and hence the subtle "I love you" message from God may go totally unnoticed to them, but not to one whose heart is seeking those words for the God that they also love.

TAKE UP SNAKES

Mark 16:18: *"They shall take up serpents."*

"There are more things in heaven and earth, Horatio, than are dreamt of in our philosophies." **Shakespeare Hamlet, Act I, Scene V.**

Shakespeare presented the character of Horatio in his play *Hamlet,* to lend creditability to the appearance of the ghost of the King of Demark, Hamlet's father who was murdered. Horatio is presented as a close friend to Hamlet, who studied together in Wittenberg and was a scholar and the embodiment of the Elizabethan skeptic of all things supernatural. For Horatio to believe he saw a ghost would make this appearance more credible to the audience. It also presented Horatio as an honest and trustworthy man who, despite his skepticism, did believe the appearance of the ghost was real when confronted with the evidence. When Hamlet told Horatio that there were more things in heaven and earth than ever dreamed of in Horatio's philosophies, he was speaking to the scholarship of his friend and telling him how little most educated people could explain away the existence of ghosts. Horatio, however, was now a believer in ghosts. The question he faced now was whether this ghost was from heaven or hell.

I can paraphrase Shakespeare by saying that there are many things in Scripture that are not dreamt of in our theologies. However, once we accept something as truly supernatural, we then must figure out if our revelation is from heaven or hell.

I remember an Arabic teacher explaining how he struggled to learn the English language. He explained how confused he was when he first came to

America and his wife was invited to a bridal shower. In his home country, where they spoke Arabic, it was a custom for the bridal party to actually bathe the bride before the wedding, and of course, he wanted to make sure his wife went to this party with plenty of soap and shampoo.

Yes, I am talking about idioms and colloquialisms. The hardest thing, for me, in the study of Aramaic is wading through all the idioms, many of which are totally lost today. Jesus spoke Aramaic and preached in Aramaic to the simple and poor people who could understand Him. Latin was spoken by Roman officials and Jews who were attached to the court of the Roman Government. Greek was understood by a few cultured businessmen and merchants. But the masses spoke Aramaic. Hebrew was only spoken in the synagogues and used as a ceremonial language. Even the Hebrew Scriptures were interpreted by the priest and Pharisees in Aramaic.

First-century Christianity was nothing more than a perfected Judaism inspired by Jewish traditions and hopes. First-century Christianity was primarily a Jewish movement appealing to Jewish racial aspirations and thought. In the second century, the Jewish Christians saw the incorporation of Greek and Egyptian traditions, and religious commercialism crept into their new Jewish movement. Doctrines and dogma were replacing the teachings of Jesus and the Jewish prophets, and there was a danger of this new, pure religion becoming assimilated into the Gentile culture and losing its Jewish identity. By the time of Constantine, many Jews dropped their interest in what was now becoming a Gentile movement. The Gospels were written for the Jews and in the language of the Jews. The style of writing and composition of the Aramaic is not easily translated into other languages. Therefore, we find Aramaic thought and manner of speech dictated into the Greek New Testament.

What this means is that the New Testament is filled with many Aramaic idioms. There are about five hundred words in the English language which have more than five thousand meanings. Now, if English, a modern language, has so many idioms and words with different meanings, then it must stand to reason that ancient languages have more idioms than English and are much more difficult to understand.

How important is it for Christians today to recognize these facts? Perhaps it could be a matter of life and death. Let's assume that the book of Mark was originally written in Aramaic and later translated into Greek. The King

James Version was translated in 1611 with little regard to the Aramaic and its idioms. Hence we have Mark 16:11 telling us: "They shall take up serpents...." I recently read where a Baptist pastor, albeit one who was uneducated and preaching in some backwoods church, demonstrated his faith by picking up a rattlesnake expecting his faith to protect him from the snake's venom. It didn't, and he died.

Would it have made any difference had he known that when the King James Version was translated, the study of sociology and linguistics was primitive at best? As a result, the translators had no way of knowing that "taking up snakes" was an Aramaic idiom that meant to unknowingly collaborate with an enemy? The picture was that when you share the Gospel unknowingly with an enemy and that enemy uses your testimony against you; you will not be harmed.

This is such a wonderful promise, except that when totally misunderstood due to lack of linguistical and sociological knowledge, it can have deadly results.

2

BROKEN – QATSA'

I Corinthians 11:24: *"And when he had given thanks, he brake [it], and said, Take, eat: this is my body, which is broken for you: this do in remembrance of me."*

Leviticus 14:34: *"When you come into the land of Canaan, which I give you for a possession, and I put a case of leprous disease in a house in the land of your possession."*

Leviticus 14:41: *"And he shall have the inside of the house scraped all around, and the plaster that they scrape off they shall pour out in an unclean place outside the city."*

I have always been baffled by this verse in I Corinthians 11:24 since I was a little child. Maybe it was just me, but I would hear this verse every time we took communion, and I would think, "How was Jesus's body broken." I mean, I heard the sermons even as a child, and I listened, and I distinctly remember hearing the preachers say that Jesus's body was not broken, they did not even break His legs as commanded by Pilate because Jesus was already dead when they came to break His legs.

The word for break in Greek is *eklasen,* which clearly means to break or be broken. Somehow the explanation that Jesus's skin was broken when he was tortured and whipped is what was meant when He said His body was broken, just doesn't seem right. To me, it appears more like this is a desperate attempt to clarify a clear contradiction. But then I read this in the Aramaic and found the word for broken was *qatsa',* which could mean to break but is usually used for scraping. In fact, it is the identical word in Hebrew and the

Targums (Aramaic version of the Old Testament) that is used in Leviticus 14:41 where the priest was to scrape the plaster of a home that was covered with the mark of leprosy.

When the people of Israel took over the Promised Land, they did not necessarily build new homes; they just took over the homes that were left by the Canaanites who fled. We learn that God sent a plague of leprosy over the Canaanites, and if one found the mark of leprosy in their homes, they were to call a priest to remediate it. Many modern translations will render this as mold or mildew rather than leprosy because it was discovered by modern medical science that a form of leprosy was caused by a certain mold or mildew.

If one found this mold in his home, he was told to report it to the priest who would come and examine it, and then if determined it was the mark of leprosy, they would shut the house up for seven days. After seven days, they returned, and if the mold had spread, they were to tear out the rocks that had the mold and then scrape the plaster off the walls. The word scrap is *qatsa'*, the same in Hebrew and Aramaic. Plaster is sort of like the skin covering the walls. Thus, Jesus could have very well been referring to His skin being scraped off by his whipping.

Jesus was likely speaking of His body having his skin scraped off for us. This would be a reference to that corruptible part of your body, that part that is continually dying and having to be replaced. You are always shedding dead skin and growing new skin. The scraping of his skin is like the bread that we are to eat, and eat all of it. Bread was a symbol of life, and through the shedding of his skin, He is passing new life unto us.

But then there is something else. Leviticus 14:34 tells us that God put this *nega' sarat* (leprosy, skin disease) on the homes. The word *nega'* not only means plague but a plague from God. It is not unusual for God to send a plague. He put leprosy on Miriam, and when she repented, God removed it. He sent a plague on Israel when they sinned by sleeping with Moabite women, and when they stopped this sin, the plague was lifted. God also sent a plague on the nation of Israel when David sinned by taking a census against the will of God. Once David repented, the plague was lifted.

Is it possible that pandemics, like the one we recently experienced upon the whole world, were sent by God? I always rejected Isaiah 53:5 as a reference to our physical illnesses. *Isa 53:5 But he [was] wounded for our transgressions, [he was] bruised for our iniquities: the chastisement of our peace [was] upon him; and with his stripes we are healed.* But let's revisit this verse and that opinion.

The word heal is *rapha'*, which means a physical healing as well as a spiritual healing. The word stripes is *chabburah* which means a wound like that from a whipping. Could it be that the scraping or *qatsa'* is a reference to both physical and spiritual? The solution to a *nega'*, a plague sent by God, is repentance. Is it possible, like the Talmud teaches, that God sends a plague as a wake-up call for us to reconnect with Him? Is it possible that maybe this recent plague that swept the world falls into the laps of us believers who need to repent and seek the face of God and reconnect with Him? After all, David pleaded with God that it was his sin and not the people who were dying from the plague that brought it about.

I could very well be wrong. Maybe God is just an opportunist and is using a pandemic to draw His people to Him. Either way, this recent pandemic did result in much repentance and reconnection with God. Maybe, that was the key to stopping the plague.

Just a thought, I could be wrong.

OUTER DARKNESS – CHOSHUKA BARI

Matthew 8:12: *"But the children of the kingdom shall be cast out into outer darkness: there shall be weeping and gnashing of teeth."*

I grew up in a fundamentalist church where there were many fire and brimstone sermons. Now I was raised to believe everything our preachers taught. They were put there by God, and I was not to question anything they taught. But there were many things I struggled with. Later in life, I was diagnosed as having Asperger's Syndrome. I was told that I did not think like most people thought. I thought more in pictures which is why I was drawn to Hebrew because it is a language of pictures. So maybe that is why I struggled with some of the sermons I heard.

One thing I could not put together that the preachers easily put together was being cast into a lake of fire which was outer darkness. Now I knew about darkness. My father would love to take us camping. I hated it because when it got dark, boy, did it get dark. There were no city lights to obscure the darkness. My father would fire up an old Coleman kerosene lantern, and as soon as that mantel caught fire, the campsite lit up. This is the picture I had of outer darkness and fire. Fire was light; darkness was no light. So what was it, were sinners cast into outer darkness or into a lake of fire which has a lot of light.

In Jewish literature that there are three types of darkness mentioned in the Old Testament. For example, *'alatah* darkness. This is a heavy darkness, the darkness that came when God made his covenant with Abraham in Genesis 15:17. This is often a word used for dusk or dawn. Dusk or dawn was often a meditative time. It was still too dark to begin or continue any type of labor, and so it was a meditative time, a time to plan your day or meditate on what needed to be done the next day. *'Alatah* is associated with a time of meditation and reflection. You do not associate evil with this darkness.

Then there was *choshke 'aphelah*, a tangible darkness which is a darkness of evil and wickedness. This is the darkness of the ninth plague. It is a supernatural darkness, like the darkness that fell on the earth after Jesus's death. For those outside the protection of God, as with the Egyptians, it was a darkness filled with terror, fear, and likely demonic beings. I often wondered what was so horrible about the darkness of the 9th plague. I mean, they had darkness at night all the time. Why should this be different? It was different because it was not just *choshke* (darkness), but *choshke 'aphaelah*, a darkness filled with terror and fear that you actually felt, a darkness that was tangible.

Then you had a darkness known as *'araphel*, which is a thick darkness. It is called thick because it is a rain cloud filled with water. Rain was considered a cleansing agent. It was dark because it was filled with water. This is found in Genesis 20:21, the cloud of God that Moses entered. The Bible said there was thunder and lightning coming from the cloud. Lightning is an electrical discharge, and an electrical discharge in the atmosphere creates ozone which you can feel and smell and creates a euphoric feeling. So this type of darkness, *'araphel*, is a good type of darkness and should properly be translated as a dark cloud. It is associated with cleansing and purification. It was in this darkness that the law of God was given to help man be purified.

But when we get to the New Testament in Matthew 8:12, Jesus taught a fourth type of darkness. English calls it outer darkness. The Greek calls it *ho skotos ho exoteron*, the Aramaic, the language Jesus spoke, calls it *chashuke bria*. This is really interesting because the word *chashuke* is similar to the Hebrew word *choshke*, which means void of light, separation from light. Only the darkness of the ninth plague uses the Hebrew word *choshke*, or darkness that is devoid of light. The other two words for darkness, which has a positive spin, do not use *choshke*. This outer darkness has no light. *Choshuke* means devoid of light, but not necessarily an illumination; it can also be a spiritual void without spiritual light or the Light of God. In other words, this is compatible with our fire and brimstone if you so wish, as it is not speaking of a lack of luminary light but the lack of the Light of God.

It is the next word that is really interesting. The word for outer in Aramaic is *bari* which is the Aramaic word for creation. This darkness is a created darkness. God is continually creating something that happens naturally. Once he removes His presence or His light, he creates a *chashuke bria*, an outer darkness, a void where He cannot be reached.

I don't know about you, but for me, the horror of hell is not fire and brimstone; it is the eternal *chashuke bria*, the darkness, the void that is created when God removes His presence. The thought of eternity separated from the God I love chills through me, which is worse than an eternal flame.

WEAKNESS - KORAH

II Corinthians 12:9: *"And he said unto me, My grace is sufficient for thee: for my strength is made perfect in weakness. Most gladly therefore will I rather glory in my infirmities, that the power of Christ may rest upon me."*

"If perfect earthly sight were offered to me tomorrow I would not accept it. I might not have sung hymns to the praise of God if I had been distracted by the beautiful and interesting things about me." **Fanny J. Crosby, poet, and writer of thousands of hymns.**

I like the way one translator paraphrased our study verse by saying: "My grace is all you need." Paul, therefore, rejoiced in his weaknesses, for the power of God rested on him. I need to examine a few words here to understand what Paul is really talking about.

The Apostle Paul could not have been a weak person in character. I mean, this old boy had one strong character, which is very apparent when you read about him in the Bible. He was not weak in decision-making, lacking courage or commitment. In that, he was powerful and strong.

Thus, this weakness has to be more than emotion or courage. I doubt it is weakness in scholarship as he was a member of the Sanhedrin and was well versed in the laws of God. The word for weakness in Greek is *astheneia* which is a physical weakness or a physical disability. The Aramaic uses the word *korih* from the root word *korah*. This also means a physical weakness, disability, or disease. This is the same word he uses when he says he will glory in his infirmities. It is my speculation that this disability was likely arthritis. However, even though that is purely a guess, it fits both Greek and Aramaic and the Apostle Paul's age.

We learn in the next verse that on top of *korah,* he also suffered insults, hardships, persecutions, and difficulties. But he rejoices in these. *Korah,* however, was different; he needed good health to carry on the ministry, not to mention to endure physical hardships. Emotionally, he could handle it, but the poor old physical body, not so much. So much so that we learn in the prior verses that he suffered a thorn in the flesh that he called upon God three times to be delivered, and each time God told Him His grace was all He needed. The word for grace in Greek is *charis,* which means a blessing, a favor, or a gift. The word is Aramaic is *yibotha,* which means exactly the same thing, a favor or a gift.

I believe that gift is found in this verse. Strength when he was weak. The word strength in Greek is *dynamos.* As we all know, it is the word we get dynamite from. But in the Aramaic, the word is *chila,* which is an accumulating of power and abilities. In other words, in his weakness, he discovered abilities and power he never knew he had.

You see, what Paul is telling us is that when we depend upon our own power and strength, we never give the power and strength of God a chance to manifest. I do not know how this power and strength were manifested, but it brought him through many difficulties.

When we face a situation that just saps us of all our strength, it is then that God can reveal what He has already endowed us with. We will never suffer more than we can bear (I Corinthians 10:13).

The key is, we don't get that strength; we already have it; it is a *yibotha,* a gift that can only be revealed when we have reached the end, when we confront our weakness, then like a supercharger, God's power kicks in. Fanny Crosby was convinced that she would not have written her beautiful songs if it wasn't for her blindness.

We, as believers, will all experience this *yibotha.* There will come a time our physical bodies will have reached their limits, and what we fear most for all our lives we will eventually confront, death's door. When that time comes, suddenly God's *yibotha* will kick in, and like Paul, we will rejoice and welcome it without the fear we thought we would have. It will be there when we need it.

5
LISTEN TO MY HEART, THIS IS MY DESTINY - ELI ELI LAMA SABACHTHANI

Matthew 27:46: *"And about the ninth hour Jesus cried out with a loud voice, saying 'Eli, Eli Lama Sabachthani?' that is My God My God, why has thou forsaken me?"*

I would like to share with you something interesting in the Easter story that many Christians find difficult to understand. There is really not much about the death and resurrection of Christ that has not been examined, debated, preached, and chewed over by scholars, so I would like to offer something interesting about the Easter story found in Peshitta. I admit my conclusions are controversial, so I present the following for your examination and consideration. I will let you decided for yourself if this has any merit.

This passage in Matthew has been debated for 2,000 years, and everyone seems to have their own explanation as to what Jesus means when he said *Eli Eli Lama Sabachthani* or *My God My God why hast thou forsaken me.*

It is curious that Matthew transliterated this into the Greek as the Hebrew *Eli*, and Mark transliterated this as Aramaic *Eloi*. *Lama* is Hebrew, *Lema* is Aramaic and is shown as that in both Gospels in the Greek, but translators will render it as *lama* (Hebrew) for whatever reason. Secondly, why did they transliterate (make a word sound the same in another language) into Greek at all? Why not just write out in Greek *my God my God why hast thou forsaken me*? As for the word *Sabachthani*, well, we are not sure what it means. It appears to be from the Aramaic word *sbq*, which means to *forsake* or *abandon for a purpose*. The Aramaic word for abandon or to forsake because it is unwanted is *taatani*. However, it can be argued that the root word is really *shwaq* which means to be *kept, spared*, or *allowed* or *to fulfill an end*. If Jesus had really meant that God had abandoned Him or forgot Him, He would have used the word *taatani* (forsake) or *nashatani* (forget).

Something even more curious is that the passage suggests that Jesus is quoting Psalms 22:1, yet in Hebrew, that phrase is *eli, eli lama 'azabethni*, not *sabachthani*. However, the Jewish Targum (Aramaic translation of the Hebrew Bible) does use the Aramaic word *sbq* in Psalms 22:1, which is probably why the scribes added the footnote, *which being interpreted means....* This is in accordance with the Eastern Church, which teaches that the scribes who wrote this out in Greek did not understand what the phrase really meant. So they merely transliterated it into Greek rather than translate it, and then put in a short commentary or their own opinion and indicated this by the words *that is to say...* In other words, they were not sure they had correctly quoted Jesus, so they assumed he was speaking Psalms 22:1 and put in a little commentary to offer their opinion as to what he really said.

Indeed Jesus could have been misquoted from scribes or witnesses at the crucifixion if they were from Judea, for the Judeans spoke a Southern dialect of Aramaic, but Jesus and his disciples were from the Northern part of Israel, Galilee, where they spoke a Northern dialect of Aramaic. So, Jesus would have spoken with a Northern accent, and sometimes what he said might not be clear to the people speaking a Southern dialect. This is probably why some thought he was calling for Elijah. My belief is that all Scripture is the inspired Word of God. It makes me more than a little uncomfortable suggesting that the Bible misquoted Jesus. If the Bible teaches Jesus said *Sabachthani,* then that is what He said, no misquotation.

Jesus spoke a Northern dialect of Aramaic. My studies have been in the middle dialect, more commonly known as the Jewish Babylonian Aramaic or Talmudic Aramaic. This is closely related to the Eastern Aramaic like the Mandaic and the Eastern Syriac of the Assyrian Church. I undertook this study so I could read the Talmud in the original Aramaic. I claim no expertise in the Old Galilean or Northern dialect. However, from my research into the Old Galilean, I find that the study of the Old Galilean is a relatively new discovery. It was felt that the Northern dialect of Aramaic or the Old Galilean dialect was a dead language. However, linguists have found a Middle Eastern tribe that still speaks this dialect, and scholars from Oxford have descended upon these people to learn some of the finer points.

This now brings us to the word *Eli*. In the Southern dialect, this would mean *my God*. However, in the Northern dialect, which is more colloquial, the word *el* would be used for more than just the word *god*; it was sometimes used in a descriptive sense. In Semitic languages, the word el simply means an authority or something that controls you. A *god* is someone or something that has control over you. People are, for instance, controlled by their heart's desires. Thus, Jesus could have been saying, *"my heart."* In Semitic languages, when a word is repeated twice, it is done to show emphasis. Hence in the Old Galilean, when Jesus said *Eli Eli*, he could have been saying, *"listen to my heart."* The word *lama (Hebrew)* or *lema (Aramaic)* generally is used as an interrogative, but this is not necessarily set in stone. To use *lema* as a question, *why am I forsaken?* or *why have I been kept?* suggests that Jesus did not understand what was happening to Him. That is not my Jesus, He is God, and He is all-knowing. In that context, we could properly and linguistically render this not as a question but as a declaration; *this is why.* In the Old Galilean *lema Sabachthani* means, *this is why I have been kept, or this is my destiny.* In fact, scholars have discovered this exact phrase is still in use in that tribe that still uses the Old Galilean. They use it in the context of *this is my destiny.* In other words, Jesus was not speaking to God, but to the people who were mourning his death, those who could understand his dialect, and in His last breath, what He could have been saying is, "*Listen to my heart, this is my destiny."* Jesus was telling those who were in sorrow over his death, *"Listen to my heart, this is why I came to earth in the first place, this is my purpose, to die for you."*

The jury is still out on this one. I am sure there are some scholars who would throw salt in the air at my conclusion, and I respect that. But if I have given you something to at least awaken you to re-examine the last words of Jesus and meditate on this the next time Easter rolls around or just meditate on it when you think of the sacrifice Jesus made. If you do that, then I am glad to suffer the slings and arrows of critics. So, let me offer this Easter message to you from just one of many understandings of the words from the lips of Jesus in His adopted native language of the Old Galilean Aramaic, *Eloi Eloi Lema Sabachthani*, which being interpreted means, *"Listen to my heart, this is my destiny This is why I came to earth in human form, and that is to die to give you eternal life."*

6

UNDIVORCED – SHEVAQ

Matthew 19:9 *"I tell you that anyone who divorces his wife, except for marital unfaithfulness, and marries another woman commits adultery."* **NIV.**

This verse has caused a lot of heartache and misery among Christians. A woman or even a man can find themselves in an abusive marital relationship, and according to the way this verse reads, the only way out is if the abusive mate commits adultery, but if not, you have to stick it out no matter how troubling, fearful or dangerous it is to live in that relationship. In that case, you should pray that God causes the spouse to commit adultery, so you have your motive to divorce.

In reading this verse in the Aramaic, I find something a little different, and I offer it to you just for your consideration.

In Greek, the word used for divorce is *apolyse,* which means divorce, release, or dismiss. The way the Greek text reads is, "And marries another commits adultery and whoever marries another who is divor*ced (apoleimenen)* commits adultery.*"* Many modern translations simply put the two *anothers* and *the who is divorced* together, making it clear that any remarriage (except in cases of adultery) is in itself adultery.

However, the Aramaic text is a little more detailed and very difficult to translate into Greek. Actually, Aramaic is very difficult to translate into any language. Still, the text in the Aramaic reads, *whoever divorces his wife without a charge of adultery.* You see, they had no-fault divorce in those days also.

Now here is where the rubber meets the road, linguistically speaking. In our English and Greek text is says *and marries another.* However, in the Aramaic text, the word *married* is not used; instead, it is the word *nasav,* which is delicately rendered as *take* but really refers to a sexual relationship. If used in an Ettaphal a causative infliction, it would mean *rape.* However, in this case, it is in a simple Pael verbal form and would more likely mean *consensual sex.*

The thinking in that day is much like today. A man is separated from his wife and planning a divorce, so he feels that he can now sleep around. Jesus is saying, "no such luck, you do not have sex outside the marriage vows." This takes it even further. Jesus is saying, "even if you are divorced, you cannot have sex until you have made vows to that woman." Premarital sex is apparently forbidden.

But we are not finished yet. Look what else Jesus says: "If you marry a divorced woman, you are committing adultery." The Aramaic says almost the opposite of what the Greek text says. The word divorce in Aramaic is *shrita,* but the word Jesus used in the Aramaic, and what is found in the Peshitta, the Aramaic text, is the word *shevaq,* which means a woman who is not yet divorced or an undivorced woman. There was the belief in that day, like today, that if a woman was separated from her husband, you could sleep with her while her husband worked out the divorce. That is what Jesus was forbidding.

In the Aramaic text, Jesus was not declaring that once divorced, you cannot remarry as indicated in the Greek text, but once divorced, you cannot sleep around. Jesus was preserving the sanctity of marriage, and that sex is to only take place within the context of marriage vows. If a man is not willing to take on the marriage vows, the commitment and responsibility of a husband with the woman he is sleeping with, he is committing adultery. If a man is sleeping with a woman who is still bound by the vows of marriage to another man, he is committing adultery. This does not mean that the vows cannot be terminated. Under the Mosaic and ancient laws, as well as the laws of our land, if two people mutually agree to break a contract, it can be broken. If one party refuses to break that contract, you're stuck. When two parties sign a divorce decree, they are no longer bound to their vows to each other either on earth or in heaven. God does not like it, but as Jesus said, Moses gave a law of divorce because of the hardness of man. God did provide a way of dissolving a marriage, but only if agreed by both parties.

The Jewish faith, of which Christianity has its roots, does allow for divorce and remarriage, and I believe Jesus would have been stoned on the spot if He really said what our Greek and English translations render His words as.

Oh, and just one more thing I would like to offer just for your consideration only. Jesus said in *Matthew 5:28: "But I say unto you, That whosoever looketh on a woman to lust after her hath committed adultery with her already in his heart."* If a woman is a very strict legalist and feels she must wait for an abusive husband to commit adultery before she can divorce him, let me just offer this, there are few men who have not committed adultery according to Jesus's definition in Matthew 5:28. God sees adultery as a matter of the heart, which most wives and husbands do. If a wife finds out that her husband is thinking of another woman while he is intimate with her, no way will you convince her that this is not adultery.

7

WOUNDED LOVE – CHAV

I John 4:18-19: *"There is no fear in love; but perfect love casteth out fear: because fear hath torment. He that feareth is not made perfect in love. (19) We love him because he first loved us."*

Do you remember your first love? For most of us, it was bittersweet. It usually happens in our pre-teen or early teen years. I remember conducting a seminar at a Sunday School Convention, and I asked those attending my seminar on teaching pre-teens how many could share a good memory of the time when they were the age of eleven, twelve, or thirteen. Most could not be sure that the memory they had occurred during that age period of their lives. In fact, many could remember very little during that age. The reason is that you forget the bad things that happen in your life, and the pre-teens years are often the most difficult years of your life. Your bodies are becoming adults while you are still being treated like children. Your hormones have gone off the charts. When I taught in Middle school, I became convinced that 75% of the hormones of adolescent girls are giggles, and 75% of the hormones of adolescent boys are show off.

It is during this time that sexuality is awakening, and you find yourself attracted to members of the opposite sex. The difference between love and sensual love is blurred and confusing. Flirting begins, and the sense of jealousy is aroused when someone also flirts with the object of your attention. That is a painful, wounding experience. You begin to dream and fantasize about a relationship with the one from whom you are seeking attention. You hardly dare use the word love; instead we call it a crush. This is a very appropriate word for the whole experience becomes a crushing experience where we experience rejection, disappointment, and a wounded heart when our fantasies don't play out the way we hope. We say our memories of our first love are bittersweet. We feel a flush of joy and pleasure when we think of our first love, followed immediately by a sense of bitterness that eventually follows.

When we consider the difference between *chav* and *racham*, we are not talking about degrees of love but the relationship involved in these words. *Racham* is a love that is pure without having been offended. This is a perfect love that has no measure, no levels; it is an equal love that is shared and can only be accomplished with God. *Chav* is a love that can move through many levels. You can love, chav, your pet dog Sparky and you can love your parents, but you do not love them both the same way. There are degrees and levels of love. A man may love a nice, greasy, juicy, cheeseburger and he may love his wife, but hopefully, there is a difference in that love. Yet, both would be defined as *chav*. *Chav* is also a love that has been wounded but continues to love. It can still be unconditional love; it can be a nurturing love, a caring love, and have all the same elements of *racham*, except like our first love, there is a tinge of sadness, bitterness to *chav*, an unpleasant memory. *Chav* has in its history a wounding and/or betrayal. Yet, the love can still be just as strong and powerful, but it is what we call bittersweet love. Still very sweet, like *racham,* but with an element of bitterness.

There is the old story of an Englishman visiting America, and when asked about the American customs, he said the thing that baffled him the most was how the Americans drank their tea. He said that they would put sugar in it to make it sweet and then lemon to make it bitter. That is sort of the dichotomy we find with *chav*. *Chav* is bittersweet. *Racham* is everything that is *chav* without the lemon or the bitterness.

Thus, we learn in I John 4:19 that "We love him, because he first loved us." In both usages of the word love, the Aramaic uses the word *'chav.* If we are talking about first love, should it not be *racham?*

The word *first* in Aramaic is the word *qadamith* from the root word *qadam*. *Qadam* has the idea of a first meeting, an initial introduction. When we first introduce Jesus into our lives, we meet Him in love. We were drawn to Him because of His love for us. Yet, when we first encountered Him and His love, his love for us was a bittersweet love. There is bittersweet, for we have that memory of our sin and transgressions. The heart of Jesus has already been wounded and broken by us. Yet, God's love for us has all the intensity of *racham*. It has all the desire and longings of *racham*. It is just as sweet as *racham* but not contaminated with the bitter memory of our sins.

It is that knowledge that Jesus still loves us even though we did break His heart. It is such knowledge that draws us into loving Him. The realization that He is willing to forgive and forget our sins and trespasses. Hence John is saying we *chav* Him in our first initial meeting. Yet, when we accept Him as our Savior and are born again, brought back into the womb, God loves us with *racham*. Yet, our inability to forget our sins, the way we broke God's heart still haunts us as it did with the Apostle Paul in *II Corinthians 12:7*: *"And lest I should be exalted above measure through the abundance of the revelations, there was given to me a thorn in the flesh, the messenger of Satan to buffet me, lest I should be exalted above measure."* It is very possible that this thorn in his flesh was not physical but mental. He was a mass murderer who killed many of the relatives of the Christians he was now ministering to. That must have surely haunted him, and the enemy used it to against him in his service to God. Paul recognized, however, that his was a thorn in the flesh, not his spirit. For once his spirit left his body, he would enter that perfect state of *racham*. But the enemy used the corruption of his flesh and/or fleshly desires to hinder him.

In the prior verse of *I John 4:18*, we learn that: *"There is no fear in love; but perfect love casteth out fear: because fear hath torment. He that feareth is not made perfect in love."* The word used here in Aramaic for love is *chav*. If we are talking perfect love, would it not be *racham*?

Yet it is the word *chav*. The word perfect in Aramaic is *mshamlya* which means perfect, mature, complete, and/or fully grown. This love will create trust, and trust eliminates all fear. The word fear in Aramaic is *dadachalatha* which is a childlike fear, the simple unreasonable fear that a child experiences. The fear of monsters under the bed, the bogey man at the window, thunderstorms, and things that go bump in the night. The child cries out in fear, and the mother or father comes in and hugs and kisses the child, assuring him that all is well. The child has such trust in the love of the parent that his fears are all cast away knowing and trusting in the complete trust that the parent loves him and will not allow any harm to come to him.

Here the word *chav* is used as this is not *racham* a pure love. The parent loves the child, unconditionally but there is a struggle in expressing the love. There is a struggle between fear and trust, and the parent must overcome the child's fear by reassuring the child of their protection. The child needs reassurance of the parents' love, where a newborn baby in *racham* has absolute assurance of the mother's love. The baby, while nursing in its mother's arms, does not for a moment question its mother's love. But when that child is fearful, and it takes reassuring from the parent, the child is in a sense questioning that parent's love, albeit in a mild way, but still the comfort does not come until that child rests in that assurance of love that he felt when just a baby. This is likely when that parent feels a tug at his or her heart that the child is growing up and even now is beginning to push away and exert his own independence. The parent begins to feel the first subtle ting in their hearts of a growing withdrawal and rebellion. It is subtle, but there is that slight hint of sadness. Racham has become *chav*. A love that has been wounded.

Yes, even that slight doubt we have in God, that slight fear that He may not protect us, tugs at his heart, wounds his heart.

LOVING SERVICE – 'AVAD

I Peter 3:1: *"Likewise, ye wives, submit to your own husbands; that, if any obey not the word, they also may without the word be won by the conversation of the wives."*

If you look up your Greek word for *submit* in an interlinear, you will discover that it is the word *hypotassomenai* from the root word *hupotasso*, which means to be of a lower rank, to be submissive or subjected to. This works in lockstep with the teachings of the church that women are inferior to men and men are the masters. A wife must obey her husband no matter what. I find it hard to believe that Peter was some chauvinistic male supremacist.

Peter spoke Aramaic and most likely had his scribe Silvanus transcribe his letter into Greek. The Aramaic uses the word *'avad*, which can have a wide range of meanings, and to put it into Greek is very difficult as you would have to make a decision as to precise nuance of *'avad* that the author intended as the Greek is a more precise language than the Aramaic.

In looking through extra-biblical literature, I find the Aramaic word *'avad* is most often used for one who *assists another person or helps another person voluntarily*. In some cases, it is used for *a servant*, rarely as a slave but more of *a bondservant*. It is used for one who loves his or her master and *willingly serves or helps the master*.

Like many Christians, I have a real problem with this *submission* business. Somewhere deep inside, I just cannot accept the idea that Peter and Paul were teaching women to subject themselves to their husbands as a slave or servant would be submissive. I just cannot accept the fact that a wife is to *submit* to her husband no matter what, as it taught in some circles. If the husband demands she not attend church, then she is obligated to not attend as she must *submit.* I cannot accept the idea that Peter meant for a woman to submit to abusive or even sexually abusive situations in a relationship.

In Ephesians 5:22, Paul says the same thing in English, "Wives submit yourselves to your husbands." Yet Paul uses a different Greek word *idiouis*. This is really a word used by most scholarly Greek-speaking people of that day. It comes from the Attica Greek used by Aristotle. Attica predated the Koine Greek of the New Testament. To Aristotle, it meant something that is *owned for its uniqueness and its specialness, like a precious gem or jewel. It is owned not for what service it could perform but because it is so desired.* I mean, a gem is just pretty and nothing else. It does not cook your meals wash your clothes etc. The owner wants to own it just because he desires it. It is possible Paul's education in Greek included a study of Aristotle, who lived some 350 years before Paul. Although Paul wrote in Koine Greek, we find that there was a great Attica Greek influence in his writings. Could it be that he did not at all intend to convey the idea that a wife was *to submit* to her husband like a slave or servant to a master but was to *be something unique and special to her husband?* He might even have been saying: "Wives make yourselves desirable to your husbands."

If that still makes you uncomfortable, then let's take a closer look at the Aramaic word, which would have been more familiar to Paul and Peter as they both used the word *'avad*, which we render as submit. As I said, *'avad* is a word used in extra-biblical literature for a bondservant or one who serves, assists, or even helps another out of love and not duty.

I am entirely convinced that God gave us the marriage relationship to demonstrate our relationship with Him. If that is the case, then Hosea 2:16 gives us the proper hermeneutical reason to reject any concept of a husband as a master: *"In that day,"* declares the LORD, *"you will call me 'my husband'; you will no longer call me 'my master.'"* Hosea could have forced his wife to serve him out of duty and fear of having her put to death for her adultery, yet that would make him a master and not a husband. He wanted, no he longed for, a wife and husband relationship, not a slave and master relationship, the same relationship God desires with us. God wants us to go to church, give offerings and tithes, keep His laws out of love, not fear, not duty, not to escape hell and earn a home in heaven, but because we love Him.

For a man to get his wife to follow him and obey him by saying, "Do it or else." is the easy way. God did not call us to the easy way and yes, even the cowardly way, neither did Peter or Paul. We have to do it the hard way, and that is getting your mate to follow you out of love and respect. That is not easy and takes a lot of work, humility, respect, and true love.

9

THE BROKEN LETTER HEI

I Corinthians 11:24: *"And when he had given thanks, he brake it, and said Take, eat: this is my body, which is broken for you: this do in remembrance of me. After the same manner also he took the cup, when he had supped, saying, This cup is the new testament in my blood...."*

It is customary in many churches to celebrate communion once a month. During this service, a pastor may quote from I Corinthians 11:24. The communion service depicts the Last Supper before Jesus was arrested. I would like to take you back to that time and offer for your consideration something that the first-century disciples might have heard Jesus say that we do not hear. Yes, I am speculating, so please keep that in mind.

Paul probably gives the most comprehensive account of the last supper. The Gospels relate this story, but they all seem to use different words. This leads many to question the accuracy of the Scriptures. However, to consider the mindset of the first-century Jewish writers, this would really not be a problem. The writers were writing the things that were most important to them personally, thus giving us a wider reporting of the events of that day.

There are also some other issues involved here. Jesus seems to really have gotten the attention of the disciples when he mentions His betrayal, but you hardly hear a peep when he talks about his death. Surely, this would have raised at least a "not so, master" or a "hold on here." However, Jesus talks about his body being broken and His blood being shed to a group who have known and grown to love Him for three years, and you hardly get an objection. Doesn't that strike you as a little strange?

Aramaic Word Study

Finally, he talks about his body being broken. His body was beaten, tortured, but Scripture makes it clear that not a bone in His body was broken. Why would He use the word broken?

Of course, these issues have been debated and discussed for centuries, and there are many possible explanations. So, I would like to throw in one such explanation taken from a Jewish point of view, just for your consideration, of course.

It is possible that when Jesus was talking about his death that the disciples were not taking Him literally. Jewish masters often teach their disciples in codes. You have the exoteric teaching, which is one everyone can understand. Jesus gives a parable, and everyone gets some sort of message from this. Then you have the esoteric teaching where the master shrouds a hidden message in his teaching that is meant only for his disciples. Thus, when Jesus *broke* the bread and said, this is my body *broken* for you….' the disciples would automatically begin decoding the secret message and would have paid little heed to whether the master was speaking literally or figuratively. The key word here could have been that word *broken*. The "Hei" is known as the *broken letter*. The *Hei* is an incomplete rectangle with a small opening in the right-hand corner. So the first letter in this game of Jeopardy is the *Hei*. Then Jesus took the cup and said, "this is my blood which is shed for you." Blood and wine are symbols of life and are pictured in the letter Yod. The sages teach that the *Yod* is the elemental, initiating force of life. They would then assume the letters were in reversed order so as to enhance its mystery, and thus they would reverse the order of the letters and have the word Yod, Hei, which would spell the abbreviated sacred name of God. If indeed the disciples were unraveling a hidden mystery, the revelation that Jesus was now officially confirming that He was Jehovah Himself. This would have bowled over many of His disciples so much that they would have given little thought to the literal expression that Jesus was going to die.

If you like this explanation, then next time you take communion, consider repeating to yourself, "This is the body and blood of Jehovah, the Master of the Universe, which was broken and shed for me."

Let's take another look at the broken letter Hei. You will notice that there is an opening in the top left-hand corner of the letter. I read in Jewish literature written about the time of Jesus that in this letter, the opening in the left-hand corner is considered the narrow gate. Also, notice at the bottom of the letter is a broader, wider opening that leads downward. This is known as the wide gate. The sages used to teach that the letter Hei represents the presence and breath of God and that it is very difficult to climb to the narrow gate and few there are who can rise to that narrow gate and achieve such a state of righteousness that they are able to pass through that narrow gate to the Shekinah or the presence of God, but many are those who pass through the broad gate that leads to destruction. We are not talking salvation here, only entering into such an intimate relationship with God that we will experience His loving presence or the Shekinah glory.

I wonder if Jesus was not making an allusion to this when He said in Matthew 7:13, "Enter the narrow gate, for the gate is wide and the road is spacious which leads to destruction, and many are those who are going in it." Just a thought.

10
THE WEDDING DANCE – CHADOTHA

Hebrews 12:2: *"Looking unto Jesus the author and finisher of [our] faith; who for the joy that was set before him endured the cross, despising the shame, and is set down at the right hand of the throne of God."*

I reserve a special time to study God's Word. I leave explicit instructions to not be disturbed during the four to five hours of personal study. There are often other things I need to do, but I just felt compelled to just sit down and study a passage of Scripture. Sometimes after about three to four hours of searching for a particular Scripture to study, I began to despair that I was wasting a lot of valuable time as I just could not feel that quickening of my spirit as I examined dozens of Scripture passages. Yet, I still feel that I must study something, and in desperation, I cry out to God: "There are a half dozen tasks that are left undone that I need to attend to if I have to live in this world. If you want me to study something in your Word, you have to show me; otherwise, I cannot sit here wasting time that I could use getting these tasks accomplished." And then an old song that I have heard as a child comes to my mind and lips. "Turn your eyes upon Jesus, look full in His wonderful face, and the things of the world will grow strangely dim, in the light of His glory and grace." – Helen H. Lemmel. This is what led me to Hebrews 12:2.

I have heard this verse many times throughout my life, but I never really meditated on it. I went right to my Aramaic Bible. I knew the Greek had a very interesting insight, but I wondered if the Aramaic would give me an ever greater depth of understanding. You see, in Greek, the word for looking is *aphorontes* from the root word *aphorao*, which has the idea of looking away from everything else to focus your gaze upon one thing. The Aramaic word is *nachor* from the root word *chor*, which is reflexive and has the idea of making oneself transparent. It is a word that you would use when a bride and groom look upon each other when sharing their wedding vows. They are committing themselves, their lives, their whole being to each other for the rest of their lives; they are promising to forsake all others, to always be there for each other, to open their hearts to each other, and keep no secrets from each other. A single English word for *chor* would be transparency. It is to look at each other with transparency.

Looking unto Jesus is not just looking at him but making yourself transparent to Him as he makes Himself transparent with you. It is like a bride and groom looking at each other as they commit themselves to each other for the rest of their lives. At that moment, they become transparent, sharing something with each other that they will not share with anyone else in the world.

The wedding motif actually carries on through this entire verse. Jesus endured the cross and the shame associated with the cross for the joy that would result from it. He did it not only for us but for the joy that the sacrifice would bring to Him, just as the bride and groom sacrifice their personal lives and their singleness for the joy of being together. Yet, that word joy is an amazing word to use here in this passage. It is the word *chadotha* in the Aramaic. This is the word used for the joyful dancing at a wedding. This again carries that wedding motif. The vows have been said as Jesus and we gaze at each other sharing our vows. We tell Jesus that we are giving Him our lives and our hearts, and now we enter that wedding feast where there is a wedding dance. In the traditional wedding dance, couples line up opposite each other. Depending on the culture and whether traditional orthodox or not, either men and women face each other or members of the same sex face each other, the symbolism still remains the same. They then move toward each other and then back away, always *chor*, gazing at each other, never taking the eyes off each other. Each time they back away, they return back to each other, only this time drawing closer to each other. This is to declare that the bride and groom will have times when they will struggle in their marriage, and they will momentarily separate from each other, but as they look *chor* or gaze at each other, they will be drawn back to each other only this time a little closer. This is what the Apostle Paul is describing in this wedding motif that we will dance this wedding dance. It is a joyful time of expressing our commitment to Jesus and He with us. Even though we may sin and draw away from Jesus, He will always keep His gaze on us, and we will be drawn back to Him only each time we return we will be drawn closer to Him. Jesus will use our human frailties that the enemy would seek to use to draw us away from Him; only Jesus will use them to bring us closer to Him.

So, we have the wedding ceremony where we gaze at Jesus in transparency, leading us to the joy of the wedding dance, and now the groom takes his place at the right hand of the Father at his *daqurasih* in Aramaic from the root word *quras*, which is a chamber with an upholstered chair or a divan, what we call a love seat, that is a chair made for two people to sit closely together. It could also be a bedroom, and the way the syntax suggests, we could read this as the bedroom in His Father's house. This is where the groom Jesus would take us His bride, to consummate our marriage to Him.

So next time you hear this verse, *"Looking unto Jesus the author and finisher of [our] faith; who for the joy that was set before him endured the cross, despising the shame, and is set down at the right hand of the throne of God."* stop and consider that the Apostle Paul might be sharing something even more intimate than the surface understanding of this verse indicates. It is also speaking of our marriage relationship to Jesus and the intimacy that He longs so much to have with us that he endured the suffering of the cross in order to obtain it.

11

MANSIONS – 'ONA

John 14:2-3 *"In my Father's house are many mansions: if [it were] not [so], I would have told you. I go to prepare a place for you. (3) And if I go and prepare a place for you, I will come again, and receive you unto myself; that where I am, [there] ye may be also."*

I have a friend who was a retired Greek teacher and priest of the Greek Orthodox church. We would get together a few times a week to study Greek and Hebrew. In his eighties, he would talk about heaven and getting his mansion. I suggested we check that verse out in the Greek and Aramaic; maybe we would get a clue as to his future mansion. After our study, he said that he is no longer expecting a mansion but something much better.

What could be better than a mansion? Well, it would not take much for me. I can barely keep my one-bedroom apartment clean, let alone a mansion. And oh, the yard work. I hate yard work. I am afraid that a mansion and all its upkeep is not a heaven I would be looking forward to.

But stop and consider how ridiculous the whole idea of a mansion in heaven is. I mean, you will not need any bedroom as there is no sleeping in heaven. You would not need a kitchen or dining room as there is no eating in heaven. You would not need a basement for a water heater, furnace, laundry, room, or storage. Why would you need a bathroom? You will not need to brush your teeth, shave, shower, and do that other thing we do now that we will not do in heaven. We would not need doors as there is no theft in heaven, nor will we need a roof as there is no harsh weather. In fact, there is absolutely no need for a house, let alone a mansion.

Oh, but everybody is looking forward to living in a mansion where they can watch the Angels baseball team play on their big screen TV in their rec room. I remember sharing the Gospel with a very intelligent guy, and he said, "You know I like the idea of a God that loves me, but you Christians are so materialistic. You accept Jesus to get a better life, to get more money, get healed, and then when you die, you get a mansion on streets of gold. I mean, really? Is that what it is all about?"

So back to the mansion idea. The word mansion in Greek is *monai,* which simply means dwelling places, rooms. Your lexicons will insert the word mansion because that is a traditional rendering but has nothing to do with the Koine Greek if you check extra-biblical sources. The Aramaic word, however, uses the word *'ona,* which sounds almost what it means in English, owner. It is a word used for a slave who has been purchased by someone and becomes his possession and finds his home with his new master. So, it means a place, but a place in a rich master's home or mansion. According to the Aramaic, we do not get our own mansion; we get to live in our Father's mansion. Only our home is not a building, but our home is wherever our master chooses to dwell. We are firmly planted in His heart as we were purchased by the blood of His Son, which puts us into His heart. Thus, we could render this as: "In my Father's house are many purchases." Those purchases are us.

But say, look at this word for house. In the Aramaic, it is *baita,* which means house, but it is also a word used in many Aramaic idioms, one being the heart. In the ancient oriental culture, as can be found today, one would say, "You are welcomed into my home." They will say that as they hold their hand to their heart to indicate that they are saying: "You are welcomed into my heart."

The fact is that there were really no mansions in the day of Jesus. When a man was betrothed to get married, he would simply add another room to his father's house. Families stayed closely together in those days and shared their dwellings.

Look at the rest of this verse and into verse 3. *"I go to prepare a place for you. (3) And if I go and prepare a place for you, I will come again, and receive you unto myself; that where I am, [there] ye may be also."* What Jesus is giving is a picture of a wedding. When a couple was married in those days, they did not live together for a year. In fact, they would likely separate for the entire year even though they were married. The idea was that marriages were usually arranged, and the couple might not have ever met before the wedding. So they were given a year to know each other without any physical intimacy. During this year's time, the bridegroom prepared an addition to his father's house, and when the year was up, he would sneak out one evening and snatch his bride away from her father's house and bring her to his house to live for the rest of her life.

Such is the picture Jesus is giving. When we accept Him as our personal Savior, we become His bride, although the marriage is not yet compensated. But Jesus is preparing a place for us in His Father's house/mansion or heaven. Then one day, He will come and snatch us away from this world and take us to His Father's house.

Here is one thing to consider. The bridegroom never sends a servant to snatch his bride away. He comes to her personally and carries her to His Father's house. When we pass from this world, it will not be an angel that will take us to heaven; Jesus will do that personally. He is our personal bridegroom.

So what can be more wonderful than a mansion? For me, what is more wonderful is to be given a place in the heart of the one who purchased me with His own blood. For me, heaven doesn't have to be a mansion. I don't want a mansion and a place where I am just reliving a physical life. I've had my fill of this physical world, and I am ready for something else, something more wonderful that our minds cannot even imagine. If a mansion to you is the best you can imagine, then go ahead and dream, my short-sighted friend, because one day you will be pleasingly surprised that you will not be met with a personal mansion but something far more wonderful that doesn't require a lawnmower and hedge trimmer.

I want to spend eternity living in the presence of the God that I am living in now. To always feel that racham, divine love. To always be where He is and to share with all His other ones the testimony of my time here on earth and the wonderful manifestations of God that I experienced and to listen to their testimonies forever.

12

DIPLOMACY – SHU'ABDA

1Timothy 2:11,12: *"Let the woman learn in silence with all subjection. (12) But I suffer not a woman to teach, nor to usurp authority over the man, but to be in silence."*

I Corinthians 14:34-35: *"Let your women keep silence in the churches: for it is not permitted unto them to speak; but [they are commanded] to be under obedience, as also saith the law. (35) And if they will learn any thing, let them ask their husbands at home: for it is a shame for women to speak in the church."*

"Diplomacy is the art of saying nice doggy until you find a big rock." **Will Rogers**

These verses are a hornet's nest, so let me say at the outset, there are many different interpretations, particularly by those much smarter than I am. So, I am only offering you my own humble take on this. I could be wrong; let the Spirit of God inside you decide as to whether my view has any merit.

The KJV makes it very clear that women are to be silent in the church and not say anything, they are not to preach or teach, and if they want to learn anything, they are to go to their husbands and learn from them. Many women have followed the literal interpretation from the KJV, and many have suffered, sometimes even abuse, because of it.

Yet, I have been blessed with the teachings of many women, and my study partner, who happens to be a woman, has blessed many with her teachings. So, my apologies to King James, but I am going with what I read from the Aramaic version of the Bible, which is Paul's native language.

First, it is indeed in Jewish law for a woman to be silent, yet in 1 Corinthians 11, you find Paul gives women full steam ahead to pray, preach, teach and prophesy in church. In the mind of first-century Christians, prophecy includes preaching and teaching. To further expand on the Hebrew and Aramaic word for prophecy, naba' also means to be ecstatic and speak ecstatically. Today we would call it a Pentecostal meltdown. If women are allowed to prophesy in church, don't expect much silence.

Either Paul is contradicting himself, or there is a matter of context here. I choose to follow the idea of context. Jewish law called women to silence only within a midrash. That is a rebuttal or discussion of a prophecy, teaching, or sermon. Unlike our churches today, we will hear a sermon or teaching where we will automatically accept it without question. We may even feel condemned for questioning the teacher or pastor. Yet, among first-century Christians as well as Jews, it was expected that all revelations and teachings be called into question and debated. Women were forbidden to participate in this for a very good reason. These debates often got very heated with disagreements. It is okay for the men to duke it out; they can usually shake hands afterward because they are not married to each other. But if the wife was present in that debate and disagreed with her husband, you are talking about an entirely different relationship. The two become one, and that means one of heart and mind. To air their dirty laundry before the congregation would not be healthy for the marriage relationship. These disagreements should be resolved at home, and the wife is to be in subjection to her husband while in church. The word subjection in Aramaic is key - *shu'abda*. The Shin is a prefix to the word *'evad*, which means a servant or one who submits. In Judaic literature, I found that as a simple Pael verb in the Aramaic so it would more correctly mean to defer to another.

There are two things to remember here, both concerning the context. The women are before the congregation; they disagree with their husbands about the sermon. Under Jewish law, they are not to voice their opinion, they are to keep silent and *shu'abda* - defer to their husbands, especially if their view is opposed to their husband's opinion. They must wait until they get home to duke it out in private.

The second thing to remember is that this is not Western culture. Oriental cultural practices this *shu'abda deferment* all the time. We call it diplomacy. I recall how our former President took on the leader of North Korea. He broke all the rules and literally insulted the leader before the world. This particular President was not a seasoned politician but a businessman, and he knew international business. Diplomacy fits the oriental way. You bow, say nice things to each other in public, and then in private, the gloves come off. The John Wayne form of negotiations is to duke it out first, and after being bloodied, you shake hands and say nice things. I cannot say for sure, but I suspect our former President refused to play on an oriental field and brought the North Korean leader on his own Western (as in cowboy) field.

My point is, it is easier to understand Paul's demand for women to keep silent if we forget all those Western cowboy movies and seek to understand the Oriental way of deference - diplomacy. Husband and wives are to share their theological disagreements between themselves and come to an understanding so that when they are with the congregation, they are not airing their dirty laundry in public.

13

WHILE REJOICING - KAD CHADA'

Acts 5:41: *"And they departed from the presence of the council, rejoicing that they were counted worthy to suffer shame for his name."*

Peter and other apostles were imprisoned by the Sanhedrin, which was ruled by Sadducees who did not believe in the resurrection, heaven, or any other type of afterlife. The afterlife is exactly what Peter and the other apostles were teaching. They were causing such a disturbance that they were tossed into prison. Well, along comes an angel who released them, and the Sadducees who thought they got rid of these radicals got word they were out preaching again. They were brought in, and after much discussion and a word from Gamaliel, who was the grandson of Hillel the Elder, one of the most respected Jewish teachers of that day, Peter and the apostles were whipped and released ordered not to preach again, an order they disobeyed. Talk about being on fire for the Lord!

I have a friend who had been a gang banger, drug addict, and dealer, you know, the whole ball of wax. We call him The Boss because of his professional wrestler size. He told how he wandered into a rival gang's area one night with his girlfriend, and they shot him two times. He tried crawling to the hospital until the police found him and took him to the hospital. It didn't take him too long to recover, and he found his way back into the gang and drugs. Until one day, he was in Humboldt Park. This is truly a bad place; you don't want to go there even on a nice sunny day. However, some preacher of a little storefront church was there, and he walked up to The Boss and said, "You wanna get off all that bad stuff? Then pray with me." Well, The Boss did, and he did. He said he was instantly released from drugs, alcohol, anger, and whatever else. You will never meet a sweeter, nicer, more loving guy than The Boss.

That was ten years ago, and he has been clean ever since. He works in a convenience store and drives his employer crazy because he witnesses to everyone who comes in. His employer won't fire him because nobody is crazy enough to work at a convenience store in that neighborhood. No one wants to mess with him because they think he is crazy. He is always waving to people, saying, "Praise the Lord." He walks the streets, stopping people and asking if he could pray for them. You know the type. Here's the point, he is at his happiest when people laugh at him, mock him or make fun of him. He just loves the Lord so much he is like Peter and the apostles. He counts himself fortunate that he is worthy to suffer shame for the name of Jesus. His boss tells him to cool it, and he just shrugs, hugs his boss, and tells him he is trying, but he just can't help himself. His boss endures it because where are you going to find another employee who has the courage to work in that neighborhood and not rob him blind.

I said he is the happiest. In Aramaic, I would use the words *kad chada'*. People laugh at him while he is rejoicing. *Kad* is the word *while*, and *chada'* is a word for being glad or merry. It is the Aramaic variation of the Hebrew word *chadah*, which is a natural joy. It is a joy expressed when you feel at peace with the entire world. It reads "while joyful." There really doesn't have to be a reason for the *chadah*, which is why the writer inserted the word *kad - while*. I see two reasons for *kad*. One is that it shows the apostles were happy even while they were being persecuted and beaten. The second, well, the very pronunciation of the words *kad Chada* is like saying "Hip Hip Hurray." It is an idiom that is used as a cheer.

I mean, who feels like cheering when people are persecuting you and beating you? The Boss does, Peter and the apostles did. Yet what do you do when someone says an unkind thing to you? You usually turn against them like ugly on an ape. But if your life is totally wrapped up in Jesus like The Boss, who cares what people think or say about you because you have *kad chada'* – while joyful or constant joy. Nehemiah 8:10 tells us that the *chadah* of the Lord is our strength.

14

BE OPEN - ETHPATHACH

Mark 7:34: *"And looking up to heaven, he sighed, and saith unto him, Ephphatha, that is, Be opened."*

Well, let's face it, Jesus has spent a long day of healing the blind, raising the dead; it is hot and dusty there in Decapolis, and now they bring a deaf-mute to Jesus to be healed. So, Jesus looks up to heaven and sighs. I don't blame Him for sighing. Another person to heal. "Hoo boy, a Messiah's work is never done." Well, I don't know why Jesus gave a *sigh*. Other translations are not much help; they all say He gave a *sigh* some will render this word as *a groan*. The Greek word here is *estenaxen,* from the root word of *stenaro*, which means to groan, sigh, mummer, complain, show grief, anger, or desire. Most commentators will say that Jesus was just expressing grief over the man's suffering. I find that a little difficult to accept as you expect him to be filled with joy over the fact that the man is about to be healed. Most commentators say that this was just a feeling of empathy or sympathy for the man. But there are other words in Greek much more appropriate to express this idea. The most common would be *klaio*. With the great love that defined Jesus, I would expect the word *odune* to be used, which expresses deep sympathy and empathy. Other words that could be used would be *katanuxis, kopetos, or lupe,* all of which would express the idea of empathy more than *stenaro*. One commentator suggested that Jesus actually began to feel the man's pain which is why He *sighed.* I tend to reject this idea as the man was a deaf-mute; he was in no pain. Maybe Jesus felt his sadness at having to endure his affliction, but again the Greek word to express that would be *lupe or odune* but certainly not *stenaro*.

Aramaic Word Study

Perhaps we might find a clue in the word *ephphatha,* which the writer or translators tells us means *be open.* There is no such word to be found in Hebrew, Aramaic, or Greek, particularly in the Northern dialect of Aramaic Jesus spoke. The word in the Northern dialect or Old Galilean for *be open* is *ethpathach.* Here may be a reason to believe the Gospels were originally written in Aramaic as it appears the Greek copyist who translated this from the Aramaic ran into some difficulty in his translation. The pronunciation and spelling of the word *ethpathach* could very easily lend itself to error. Such errors would not occur in our scientific and precise cultural setting of today. Our linguist would have tools today that would be unavailable to the copyist of the first century. Nor were the copyists serving as translators subjected to the rigorous demands of the scribes of the first century who copied the Torah. These scribes only copied the Torah; they were not expected to translate. Many scribes were not even translators; they were just secretaries who wrote up letters for those who could not write. Possibly, the copyist who translated the works of Mark into Greek could very well have been unfamiliar or fluent in the Old Galilean dialect of Aramaic. They most likely made their translations through dictation and could have easily heard and written down *ephphatha* rather than *ethpathach,* and then when they translated, they could not be sure of the proper rendering of the word, which is why they just simply transliterated it and followed it up with their understanding of what the word was to mean.

The same could be said for the word *sigh,* which in the Aramaic is *noach* and is very similar to the Aramaic word *noohra (light).* If given either orally or in writing, confusion could occur. In the Madhya or Eastern script, I could see how a copyist would confuse the Resh for a Chet. Still, the free-flowing and ambiguous nature of the Aramaic language makes it very difficult to render certain words and phrases into an exact language like Greek or English. Hence you have about 26 occasions when the copyist transliterates a word from the Aramaic. He does this as he realizes that his Greek rendering would not be an adequate translation.

Noach in Aramaic, as in Hebrew, is a difficult word to translate. It literally means to rest. When used as a *sigh,* it represents the idea of giving a sigh when you sit down after a long journey. But there is more built into that word that you cannot express in English or Greek. *Noach's* close association with the word *Noohra* in the Aramaic would suggest God carefully chose the word when He inspired Mark to write it down. In its most Semitic form,

Noach has the idea of a physical manifestation or release of something inside a person, usually a type of passion. Hence you get the rendering of a *sigh* as the *sigh* in a physical expression of something you feel, either weariness, frustration, or even anger. Using the word *Noach,* Mark was expressing the fact that at the moment Jesus looked up to heaven, there was a physical manifestation of something coming out of Him. The close association with the word *Noohra* leads me to believe what Mark is expressing is that the people witnessed some sort of light emanating from Jesus as he spoke the word *ethpathach.* That is just my speculation, and I could be wrong.

But there is something I am not wrong about, and that is that the word *noach* does mean an expression of something inside of you. Call it a *sigh* if you wish, but I prefer to call it an expression of the heart. It was an expression of the heart of Jesus that healed this man. Jesus healed this man with a *sigh (noach or an expression of His heart).*

Whenever I attend any speaking engagement, my number one theme is to encourage believers to study the Word of God, to pray, and to mediate with their hearts, not with their minds. For it is with the heart that you believe and are justified, it is with your mouth that you confess and are saved – Romans 10:10. Western Christians spend too much time studying the Word of God with their minds; they pray with their minds, they worship with their minds. It is time we learn to think like a Hebrew and study, pray and worship with our hearts. When you pray for someone to be healed, you must pray with your heart, just as Jesus prayed for this man with his heart. We must also *sigh (noach) or* allow our hearts that are joined with the heart of God and let that power emanate from us.

How do you know if you are using your heart or mind? Your pet dog Sparky will know. Hold your pet's head in your hand and stare him in the eyes (dogs hate that), and say, "I love you." If he does not try to fight you or turn away, he will know you are speaking with your heart and not your mind. (I bet I will have a dozen vets write me and tell me I am wrong).

DIVINE LOVE – RAV CHESSED

John 13:35: *"By this shall all [men] know that ye are my disciples, if ye have love one to another."*

In Aramaic, the word used in this verse for love is *chava'*, which means love, as well as other English words like to cherish, which is simply another expression of love. We hear this word love all the time among groups we participate with. I had a Jehovah's Witness tell me the reason she belonged to the organization is that everyone loves each other. Then she pointed to John 13:35 as proof she belonged to the one true faith because they love each other. I mean, everybody today belongs to some group or organization where they get together and love each other. Christians get together and love each other, veterans get together and love each other, Peta gets together and love each other as they love their animals, even left-wing radical socialists get together and love each other, for crying out loud. So, what is the difference? How are people to tell if we are truly His disciples when we love each other like the inebriated patrons in the bar down the street love each other?

The word *chava'* from the root word *chav* is a word used for all kinds of love. I don't see where Jesus pointed out anything special about this love, only that it would prove they were His disciples. So once again, I started to search through Jewish literature to see if the first-century disciples heard something that we don't hear, and I think I found it.

Among Orthodox Jews, there is the belief that there are two types of love: the *Rav Chessed* and *Chessed Olam*. *Rav Chessed* is attributed to Aaron. Aaron's name is really from the Middle Egyptian, meaning a mountain of strength. But this is a spiritual strength that was special to Aaron. The sages called it *Rav Chessed*, Great Mercy of love, or Master of Mercy of love, but the intent is Divine Mercy or love. The love of God flowed through Aaron. Aaron was the first Hebrew priest to possess this love. The letters to Aaron's name are Aleph, Hei, Resh, Nun. The sages teach that this also spells out the Nir'ah, which means a visual representation of something unseen. In other words, Aaron was a visual representation of the love of God. This gift was said to be passed down through the generations of priests and is even seen today among members of the tribe of Levi.

This is more than just expressing the love of God. They had the ability to confer the aura of love on a group and nation. When Paul said in I Corinthians, "faith, hope, and love but the greatest is love," I believe he was referring to *Rav Chessed*. A Divine Love which can be conferred upon others who are willing to receive it. We say people have a spiritual gift of preaching, teaching, music, etc. We rarely hear of someone with the greatest gift, the gift of love or the gift of being able to bestow love, to bring love to a group of people or a situation.

There is another love called *Chessed Olam*; this is an earthly love, a natural love. I believe the disciple hearing Jesus say that they will know we are Christians by your love for one another knew He was referring to *Rav Chessed*, a love that they passed on to each other and to the rest of the world. It was a love they could not generate on their own; it was a natural divine love that came from the very presence of Jesus living inside of them. It was that gift of love that ability to pass on the Love of God.

Did you ever met a person and just somehow know they belonged to God, even before they spoke? I remember years ago, a friend of mine went to the old Soviet Union when it was under Communist rule, and it was a crime to be Christian. He was sent by a mission board to make contact with the underground church and find out what American Christians could do to help them. He knew very little Russian and could hardly read it. He had no idea how he could find a Christian, but he just believed God would lead him to them. He was riding on a bus when a young man sat in another seat facing him. He was smiling. That was his first clue; nobody smiled in that atheistic country. The American Christian smiled back, and then the young Russian reached into a plastic bag and held out some papers. The little Russian my friend knew was enough to recognize these as handwritten copies of Scripture verses. Bibles were forbidden, but someone had a Bible, and they painstakingly hand-copied portions of Scripture. My friend smiled and handed the papers back to the young Christian who held those papers to his breast as if they were his very soul. Then this young Russian handed him a book. The American recognized this book as a hymn book. He could not read Russian, but he could read the music. It was that hymn "How Great Thou Art." The American began to sing it in English, and this young Russian man just began to weep. The American wanted to give him his Bible, but the Russian said in broken English, "No, I cannot be seen taking anything from you." He then got up to get off the bus, but before he did, he reached out and hugged this American Christian and said: "I can never see you again, but I will see you again, one day I will see you again." He then walked off the bus. That was fifty years ago; they likely have never met again. But one day, they will, they will meet again.

They will know we are Christians by our *Rav Chessed* for each other.

16
RICH AND POOR – 'ATAR MASAK

II Corinthians 8:9: *"For ye know the grace of our Lord Jesus Christ, that, though he was rich, yet for your sakes he became poor, that ye through his poverty might be rich."*

I grew up hearing this verse over and over in sermons and on Christian radio. I rarely, if ever, most likely never, heard anyone explain this verse. I guess they just assumed that everyone would naturally understand its meaning—everyone except Chaim Bentorah. Maybe I did, but it never made sense to me.

Why would Jesus need to be rich? How could He become poor when He was God incarnate? Now before you start saying this is a reference to spiritual richness, I must ask you what spiritual richness is? To me, the only richness that is spiritual is a closeness to the Heavenly Father. The closer you are, the richer you are spiritually. I am good with that, except Jesus was God. How could He get any closer to Himself? I know, this Chaim Bentorah really has problems. On top of that, the Greek word used for rich in this verse is in its root form *plousio*, which is a reference to material wealth. The word in Greek for poor and poverty is *ptocheia* which is begging, poverty destitute, again a reference to lack of material wealth nothing spiritual about it.

Commentators have given many plausible explanations. The one I like the best is that Jesus paid off our debt of sin, but it cost Him everything to do it. However, as a result, we became rich spiritually by becoming children of God who owns everything. I know it has a few rough bumps and is not really true to *plausio* and *ptocheai*, but I like it.

However, I checked this out in the Aramaic and found some interesting things. First, the word for grace is *tivutah* from the root word *tov* which means to be in harmony with God. Thus, right away in the Aramaic, I would read this *as "For you know that in order to be in harmony with us, even though he was rich...."*

Okay, let's take that word rich apart. In Aramaic, in its root form, it is *'atar*. Now, if this were Hebrew, it would mean to press strongly toward a goal. The word moved into the Aramaic during the Babylonian captivity, where the Babylonian merchants sought the services of the Hebrews because they displayed a unique talent for business and making money. As a result, the Hebrew word *'atar* moved into the Aramaic as a word for striving toward a goal to become wealthy. However, we must remember that wealth in those days, as it is today, meant power. Paul is most certainly using money or material wealth as a metaphor, but a metaphor to symbolize power. Jesus left a position of ultimate power, rich in power if you like for our sakes to become poor and through this poverty, we will become empowered.

The word for poor in its root form is *masak*. This is also a Hebrew word that got itself intermixed with the Babylonian Aramaic. In fact, that is what the word means in Hebrew is to mix together. During the Babylonian captivity, the word moved into Aramaic with the idea of mixing together in order to reduce. Another word is to consolidate. A key business move is to consolidate your business and reduce your overhead. You make your business leaner and meaner. When Jesus came to earth, He consolidated His power. He took all the power of God and put it into a human body. When a business is consolidated, it is no longer a big overstuffed business but has had all the fat and dry wood removed so that it is a smaller, more profitable business and the goal of any business is to show a profit.

When Jesus came to earth as a human being, He trimmed all the fat out of our obligation to God. No longer was it necessary to offer sacrifices and offerings to God. He cut out all the red tape and simply said, "Just believe in Me, and you will have eternal life." Everything the Torah law required was fulfilled in Jesus Christ. The offerings, the sacrifices, the commitments to follow a complex list of dos and don'ts reduced to simply accepting Jesus as your Savior and learning to love Him with all your heart, soul, and might. When you come to realize the price He paid to come to earth and suffer torment, pain, and death just so we can be in harmony with Him, is that not enough to motivate you to love Him?

Not only that, but we do not have to do a thing to become worthy to enter a harmonious relationship with God. Jesus did it all and what we have to do is just surrender our hearts and lives to Him, and He gives us His heart and eternal life. In fact, the Aramaic word for *you* is *'anthun*. Turn the Aleph into a prefix, and you have the word being God giving you. We don't earn one snippet of our redemption, salvation, or eternal life. It is given to us, and we just accept it.

Grace, undeserved favor is written all over this verse. In fact, it is what this verse is all about.

TONGUES OF FIRE LASHANA NORA'

Leviticus 6:13: *"The fire shall ever be burning upon the altar; it shall never go out."*

Leviticus 9:24: *"And there came a fire out from before the LORD, and consumed upon the altar the burnt offering and the fat: [which] when all the people saw, they shouted, and fell on their faces."*

Acts 2:3: *"And there appeared unto them cloven tongues like as of fire, and it sat upon each of them."*

"Although a fire descended from heaven upon the altar, it is a commanded to add to it a humanly produced fire." **Talmud Eruvin 63a**

Why was there a command to keep the fire that fell from heaven going? The Jewish sages such as Alshich taught that the fire was a symbol of God's love. A human element was needed to keep the fire going, and it was a discipline to make sure that the fire was never extinguished. Fire has always symbolized passion, both good and bad. Many times, God would send fire from heaven as a sign of his passion for justice, as with Sodom and Gomorra. He would send fire from heaven to consume an offering to show his passionate love. Even in administering judgment, He is showing His passionate love for those who have been wronged.

The word itself tells us of God's passion. It is one of the rare words that does not have a three-letter root. It is spelled, Aleph Shin. The Aleph represents God, and the Shin represents a consuming passion. Fire is representative of God's consuming passion.

God sent a fire from heaven to consume the offering on the altar. He commanded that this fire be kept burning. Certain priests were ordered to keep a daily watch over this fire to make sure it never went out. Every morning there was a ceremony performed by the priest to add some fuel to the fire to keep it going. The Talmud is teaching that God commanded the fire to be kept going by a human element to show that His love upon this earth is meant to be shared by mankind.

Amy Carmichael was a missionary to India at the turn of the 20th century who found herself saving young girls and women who were forced into prostitution by the Hindu temple to earn money for the priest. She began her work with these temple children when a young girl named Preena escaped from the temple and sought shelter with Amy Carmichael. Amy Carmichael withstood threats against her life by those who insisted Preena be returned to continue her sexual assignments. Someone once asked her what missionary life was like, and she replied: "Missionary life is a chance to die."

When Preena was asked what drew her to Amy Carmichael, she said that she saw the light of the true God. Other children who escaped to find refuge with Amy Carmichael also said it was love that drew them to Amy. These children were drawn to Amy Carmichael by love. These were children given by desperate parents to the temple to serve as prostitutes in hopes that the gods would bless them. They feared these gods. In fact, you look at most religions in the world, and they fear their gods. They give offerings and sacrifices out of fear that their gods would harm them in some way if they did not show their devotion. The God of Amy Carmichael was a God of love, and they saw it in her life and in the case of Preena in actual light.

The fire did go out in the temple during the destruction of the temple in 586 BC by the Babylonians under King Nebuchadnezzar. The Talmud would teach that the fire would not return to the temple until the Messiah came, was tortured, put to death, and resurrected. Then after he would be glorified in heaven on the day of Pentecost, the fire would return. In Acts 2:3, we learn that on the day of Pentecost, after Jesus returned to heaven to be glorified, the Holy Spirit descended in tongues of fire. The word *tongue* in the Aramaic is *leshana* which really means *language*. The believers were filled with the Holy Spirit and began to speak with a language of fire. Remember, the word fire is symbolic of passion. They began to speak with a language filled with the passionate love of God. It also says they spoke with *peleg*, which is to *separate and divide*. They spoke with a language that was separated and divided from themselves. It was a language or speech coming right from God.

Once again, the fire was lit. Paul says our bodies are the temple of God, and when we receive the Holy Spirit into our bodies, the temple, we carry that fire of God, but yet Leviticus 6:13 commands us that we are to keep that fire from going out through a human effort. It is our job to keep that fire going in us through our acts of love for God such that people will see it and not us as it was with Amy Carmichael.

Many years ago, as a college student, I attended the Urbana Missionary conference in Urbana, Illinois. It was a gathering of thousands of Christian college students who were challenged to become missionaries. On the closing night, we all gathered in the stadium at the University of Illinois Urbana. We were each given a candle, and at the close, ushers lit the candle of a person sitting at the first seat in a row, and that person would light the candle next to him. The lights were turned out, and in a few moments, the entire stadium was lit by candlelight as we all sang:

> It only takes a spark
>
> To get a fire going
>
> And soon, all those around
>
> Can warm up in its glowing
>
> That's how it is with God's love.'
>
> Once you've experienced it
>
> You spread His love to everyone
>
> You want to pass it on.

Israel stopped passing the fire, the consuming passion of God, around, and when they did, the fire went out. God has placed a fire, the fire of His consuming love in us, His temple, but like the priest of old, we have to daily make sure that fire is fed. Unless we share that love, it will go out, and we will just be faking it but fooling nobody.

18
THE (THIRD) TEMPLE - BEIT HAMIQADASH

II Corinthians 12:2-4: *"I knew a man in Christ above fourteen years ago, (whether in the body, I cannot tell; or whether out of the body, I cannot tell: God knoweth;) such a one caught up to the third heaven. (3) And I knew such a man, (whether in the body, or out of the body, I cannot tell: God knoweth;) (4) How that he was caught up into paradise, and heard unspeakable words, which it is not lawful for a man to utter."*

"Because very soon, when Moshiach (the Messiah) comes, we will experience these great expressions of love and connection with God. You will know and understand. All this will come with the Beit Hamiqadash (the third temple). However, it only becomes the Beit Hamiqadash (third temple) when it is completed and descends (from the heavens) with the coming of Moshiach (the Messiah) in the clouds" - **Torat Habayit, Sefer Hamaamarim 5689 p. 189.**

I am surprised to learn how few Christians know that back in 1948 when the United Nations was debating over creating the State of Israel, believe it or not, there was a strong contingent of Jews who opposed the establishment of the Jewish nation. Their reasoning was clear; only the Messiah could bring in the nation of Israel when he descends in the clouds. Further still, I am surprised that many Christians are unaware of the same contingent, who still oppose the establishment of Israel as a nation also oppose the building of the third temple.

The reason behind this is just as clear. For one thing, it is believed that even before the building of the second temple, Ezekiel prophesied the building of another temple. There are a number of Scriptures that allude to the third temple or the *Beit Hamiqadash*. The word *beit* means house or place of dwelling, and the *Hamiqadash* comes from the root word as *kodesh*, which means holy with the definite article *Ha*. For The Holy Place of Dwelling. During the days of Jesus, there was much debate over the legality of the second temple, and it came as no surprise to many when Jesus spoke of the destruction of the temple. In fact, that is why He created such row when He spoke of it. Many zealots of the Jewish faith actually plotted to destroy the temple, and when Jesus mentioned the destruction of the temple, He was automatically identified as one of these traitors.

Pilate was well aware of the dissension among the Jewish community and the right-wing radicals who were plotting to destroy the temple because they felt it was illegitimate as it was not built by the Messiah, which is why Pilate was not too anxious to arrest Jesus. He considered Jesus to be on the side of the Roman Government who wanted to destroy the temple.

There was good reason for these hard feelings toward the second temple. The rebuilt temple was clearly outlined in Ezekiel 43, but the instructions for the next temple were incomplete. The Jews went ahead and built it anyway without the complete plans. When it was completed, the presence of God did not dwell in the second temple like the first. The Holy Spirit was not in the second temple, nor was the Ark of the Covenant in the second temple like the first. Many Jews believed that the Messiah would come to complete those portions of the temple not found in Ezekiel 43, and they argued to wait for the Messiah before completing the second temple. But instead of leaving it uncompleted to await the final instructions from the Messiah, they went ahead and built it according to the plans of the first temple.

Now today, once again, the Jews are pushing to rebuild the temple, although they do not have the exact specifications for the third temple, the *Beit Hamiqadash*. If not built according to exact instructions, it will not serve as a Holy Place of Dwelling for God.

Okay, there is more, but what I want to say in this short study is that Paul visited the third heaven. The word in Aramaic for heaven is very similar to the Hebrew yet has a shade of difference. It is the word *shami'a*, which means joyous, happy, and peaceful. It comes from the same root as Simchas, which means rejoicing.

Here is what I am finding. There is a teaching among Jews about seven levels of heaven, which other Christians and I do not believe, and neither do many Jews. But what do we do with Paul saying he visited the third heaven? I am finding that among a strong segment of Jewish teachers, the third heaven is synonymous with the *Beit Hamiqadash*, the Holy Dwelling Place of God, or the third temple. As a good Jew and one who was trained in the depths of Jewish teaching, Paul was well aware of the expression of the third heaven as a reference to the true temple of God that was being prepared in the heavens. Those who rejected the second temple anticipated its destruction, and a third temple was being prepared in the Heavens. Note that the word heaven is always found in a plural form in both Hebrew and Aramaic.

Note also, in the fourth verse, Paul also visited paradise or *paradis* in the Aramaic, which means a pleasure garden and is believed to be the abode of the righteous until the resurrection. It is considered a place of truth. In other words, the third heaven and paradise are two different places, with the third heaven being the third temple. When God recreates the earth, according to this Jewish teaching, the third temple will come down to earth, the Garden of Eden be revealed again, and the earth will become the Garden of Eden once again for all who are righteous or in Christian lingo, those who have accepted Jesus as their Savior.

By the way, these Jews also believe that *paradis*e is the Garden of Eden which exists in another realm or what we call another dimension. It exists alongside us right now in another dimension, so to speak, like a parallel universe. It is where the righteous go after death or, again in Christian lingo, those who have accepted Jesus as their Savior will go when they die, we call it heaven.

Will the Jews build a third temple? They will not build the third temple that is the temple that will be a true Holy Dwelling Place for God. Only the Messiah can build that temple, for only He will know the correct dimensions and style it is to be built. Now there might come a fellow who will convince the Jews he is the Messiah and will erect a temple. Watch out for this old boy because if he successfully builds a temple, He is not the Christ or Messiah; he is an anti-messiah or antichrist.

19
O YOU OF LITTLE FAITH - 'ANATHON ZE'ORI HIMANUTHA

Matthew 8:25-26: *"And his disciples came to [him], and awoke him, saying, Lord, save us: we perish. (26) And he saith unto them, Why are ye fearful, O ye of little faith? Then he arose, and rebuked the winds and the sea; and there was a great calm."*

Matthew 14:30-31: *"But when he saw the wind boisterous, he was afraid; and beginning to sink, he cried, saying, Lord, save me. (31) And immediately Jesus stretched forth [his] hand, and caught him, and said unto him, O thou of little faith, wherefore didst thou doubt?"*

Some stories are so familiar; we have heard these stories in countless sermons and in Sunday School that we really don't need to read them from Scripture. A common mistake Christians make. They read the Bible, see a familiar story and just scan over it as they are certain they know this story. But let's just pause and really look at a couple of aspects of these two stories.

In the first story, the disciples are in a boat with Jesus at sea. A storm comes up, and the disciples are desperate. They go to Jesus and say: "Save us, we perish." Jesus asks them why they are afraid and then apparently scolds them for having such little faith. In the second story, Peter walks on the stormy waters but begins to sink and cries out, "Lord save me." Again Jesus rebukes Peter for having such little faith.

Here's my question. When the disciples asked Jesus to save them in the first story, what made them think Jesus could do anything about a storm? It seems to me they had a whole lot of faith in Jesus to believe He could rescue them from a storm. But when Jesus calmed the sea, they were amazed. Well, what did they expect Jesus to do? Turn the boat into a speed boat and rush them ashore? Maybe pick them all up and fly them through the air? Well, to be fair, when I call out to Jesus to help me, I don't have any idea how He is going to get me out of the mess I got myself into, and I am also amazed at how He does it. But at least I had enough faith to call out to Jesus. To accuse the disciples of having little faith when they actually called upon Him to rescue them? That doesn't seem to be a teaching moment.

Then we have the story of Peter, who jumps over the side of the boat and walks out to Jesus on the water. He must have gotten close enough to Jesus before he started to sink, as all Jesus had to do was reach out and grab him. I mean, that is not a "little" faith; that is whole bunches of faith. Yet, poor Peter is scolded for having little faith. When Jesus lifted him out of the water, his faith must have been restored, as we don't read about him sinking again.

So why was Jesus scolding them with, "Oh, you of little faith." I mean, like He is absolutely disgusted with them. But, who says Jesus was scolding them? In Greek, that exclamation "oh" is not found in the text; it is simply "You of little faith." The word little in Greek is *oligos*, which means small in number or quality. The preposition "of" is not there either and could be rendered as "You have little faith" or "You have a little faith." The Aramaic is a bit more clear. The word for little is *zeora* with no exclamation "oh." Church tradition sticks that "Oh" in there, which has no business being there except that the translator and the church which sponsored the translators wanted it to be there to provide good sermon material on how we need to build our faith and why miracles do not happen. It is simple; we have little faith, shame on us.

Zora could mean little, but that is misleading. The word really has the idea of someone who is young and inexperienced. It is used for an apprentice who has not yet mastered a certain skill. Literally, in Matthew 8, Jesus is making a statement. It is in a simple Peal form. "Your faith is yet quite young." The implication is: "Why are you afraid? You have faith, it is young and inexperienced, but you do have faith." He told the same to Peter: "Peter, you are inexperienced in faith, but doggone it, you have faith, why doubt?"

Remember what Hebrews 11:1 says in Aramaic: "Now faith is the substance of what you can imagine and the revelation of what you cannot see." Peter imagined He was walking on water, and indeed he was. It was the revelation of what he could not see. Once he looked at the angry waves, he started to imagine himself sinking, and he began to sink.

One other thing. Jesus used the Aramaic word *lemana,* which could mean why but could also mean "to which or but." In other words: "You have a young inexperienced faith, and yet you walked on water, how great is that? But then you let fear cause you to doubt." He told the disciples the same thing. "You have a young and inexperienced faith, yet you came to me for help believing I could do something, but you let fear cause you to doubt, to break your concentration on your imagination, letting that computer in your head tell you, 'Yeah, Jesus is powerful, but this situation is impossible,' then doubt came and you panicked."

Are we not guilty of the same thing? We have an immature faith, but we have enough faith to call out to Jesus to help us in times of trouble, imagining that He will help us and we may, even like Peter, walk out our faith but as soon as we let that old computer in our head start reasoning this all out: "You know, Bunkie, this is impossible, I personally don't see how Jesus is going to get you out of this." You then begin to doubt. The biggest mistake we make is like the disciples and Peter; we try to figure out how Jesus will help us and when we start doing that, we conclude it is impossible. Like the disciples call out to Jesus for help but conclude they were in an impossible situation or Peter actually walking out his faith and then suddenly thinking: "Wait a minute, I am walking on water, this is impossible."

You sink, and then you blame Jesus or blame the idea that you don't have enough faith. If you have enough faith to imagine God helping you, you have enough faith. Don't let that computer in your head tell you otherwise.

20
APPLAUSE – SEPHAQ

II Corinthians 3:5: *"Not that we are adequate in ourselves to consider anything as coming from ourselves, but our adequacy is from God."*

When I hear the word adequate, I think of something that barely passes. When I was teaching, I considered a "C" grade as adequate, just about average, maybe a little below. So, I read II Corinthians 3:5, which tells me that my adequacy is from God. Is that all God is going to give me to do His work? Just adequate? The word adequate in Greek is *hikanoi,* which means to be sufficient, competently strong, worthy, or suitable. That sounds a little better, but I do like the Aramaic word that is used much better, which is *sephaq.* It is a word used for the striking of hands at an event; in short, it is applause. Now read this verse using our English word applause: "Not that we receive applause for ourselves to consider anything as coming from ourselves, but our applause is from God." I believe the story I wrote about Sylvia Pig when I was paying my way through college as a ventriloquist explains this verse quite adequately (there's that word again)

If you were to visit Uncle Otto's farm, you would be impressed by how well kept and maintained his farm is. Everything is in good repair, the grass is mowed, and it really is well-tended except for one small area, the pigpen. Grass never grows in the pigpen. In fact, even in the driest weather, the pen is still just one big mud puddle. The reason is that pigs love to roll in the mud and then just lay in the sunshine and let that mud bake on their backs.

Now the pigs were not the only ones who appreciated the sunshine. King, Uncle Otto's white stallion, is well aware that all the grass, hay, and alfalfa he eats would not be possible if it were not for the sunshine. The chickens know to lay their eggs when the sun comes up, and Baby Doll, Uncle Otto's milk cow, knows it is time to give milk when the sun comes up. Yes, indeed, all the animals know the consequences if there should be a morning that the sun does not rise. For this reason, they live in mortal fear that Rooster, their sun prophet, would one day not crow.

For you see, every morning when Rooster crows, the sun comes up. Therefore, by animal logic, Rooster crows, the sun comes up; therefore, Rooster makes the sunrise.

Well, let us jump to our story about Silvia Pig. Silvia was not as large as the other pigs, as pigs go. She did not smell as foul as the other pigs. Worst of all, Silvia's oink was unlike the oink of the other pigs. It was sort of high-pitched, squeaky-like. Silvia just did not match up to the other pigs by the pig criteria that would exalt a pig in pigdom. However, she loved to roll in the mud and let it bake in the sunshine just as much as the other pigs, but alas, the other pigs paid Silvia no mind. She was often shunned to the remotest part of the pigpen, usually in the shade where there was little mud and little sun.

"Oh," bemoaned Silvia. "If only I could do something really great, really important. Something that would make me special in the eyes of the other pigs." Silvia would dream of some great exploit, doing something very heroic and all the pigs praising her and Bruno Boar fawning over her, giving her his spot in the muddiest and sunniest part of the mud puddle that Bruno reserved only for his favored pigs.

One morning Silvia observed Rooster as he crowed to call the sun up in the morning and began to think. Now you must realize that pigs are of such little brain that they often think things that seem strange to us who are of more brain. Silvia began to wonder why the sun would listen only to Rooster's crow and no one else. Maybe it was his special voice. Maybe, yes, not maybe, but a fact that Silvia's strange oink was not a curse but a gift. A gift to call up the sun every morning.

My friend, when one thinks a fantasy about herself, before long, she begins to believe it Soon Silvia began to puff herself up and share with the other chickens her new revelation about herself. She was indeed a sun prophet, ordained to be a backup to Rooster. She was the prophet in waiting. If Rooster ever failed to crow, she, with her gifted oink, would call the sun up.

Well, of course, all the other pigs laughed and mocked Silvia. For even though pigs have little brain, they knew enough to know that Silvia indeed had more bacon than pork.

But one morning, the animals on Uncle Otto's farm faced their worst nightmare. Rooster lost his voice. He had a bad cold. Instead of a bold **"cockle doodle doo,"** All that came out was a pitiful "cockle doodle doo." "Oh," mooed Baby Doll, "The sun will not rise, how will I ever give my milk" "Or our eggs," clucked chickens, "I will have no hay," Whinnied King. Yes, and even Bruno Boar showed signs of panic: "My beautiful mud hole will not be soft and moist." Oinked Bruno Boar mournfully.

"Quick," said Baby Doll to Buddy, "Go get Uncle Otto's cough medicine." "I'm on it!" barked Buddy. Now, Uncle Otto used to make his own cough medicine. The word for Uncle Otto's cough medicine comes from the same root word as Moonshine. But, hey, it worked for Uncle Otto. It will surely work for Rooster.

Rooster began to sip Uncle Otto's cough medicine. It burned as it went down. "That means it's working," snorted King hopefully. "Yes," said Pigs, "It is burning away that nasty cold that keeps Roosters cockle doodle doo quiet.

However, Rooster did not look too good after drinking Uncle Otto's cough medicine. In fact, it appeared he had problems standing. "Go ahead," encouraged Baby Doll to Rooster, "Give it a try." Rooster fluffed himself up, staggered a little, and let out: "Cock, hic, a, hic, do, hic a hic doooooooooooooooooo!" He was out cold. "Oh," moaned the farm animals, he will never wake up now to call the sun. We are doomed, doomed!."

In walked "Silvia. "You need not fear, my friends, for I have been gifted with a special oink. I have studied oink in the best pig pens in the country. I studied under the world's best oink prophets. I even studied in the School of Oink. I know how to call the sun up." Well, all the animals knew Silvia was never at any other pig pens, but this was not a time to argue. It was worth a try. Desperate times called for desperate action. They quickly led Silvia to Rooster's fence post and left her there to call up the sun as each farm animal took their usual morning positions.

"What have I done?" thought Silvia, "What if the sun does not arise. Oh, how the farm animals will laugh at me." But Silvia had no choice, and maybe this was fate. So she gave it her best oink. "Oink di oink oink." And you know what, dear reader? The sun did come up, shining as bright as ever.

"She did it, praise to Silvia, she oinked the sun up." Shouted all the farm animals. All the animals gathered around Silvia, praising and honoring her as a truly gifted pig with a gifted oink. Silvia just beamed. Then Bruno Boar stepped forward. "Come, little Silvia. Come share my mud puddle with me in that nice hot sun you oinked up." Silvia's dream had come true, and that afternoon as King and Baby Doll walked by the pigpen, there they saw Silvia laying in the muddiest and sunniest part of the pigpen. "Yes, " said King, "Silvia is truly a pig in the sunshine."

II Corinthians 3:5: *"Not that we receive applause for ourselves to consider anything as coming from ourselves, but our applause is from God."*

21
EMBRACE OF SUFFERING – CHASHA

Hebrews 4:15: *"For we have not a high priest which cannot be touched with the feeling of our infirmities; but was in all points tempted like as [we are, yet] without sin."*

This is one of those verses that we just cannot get the real depth of understanding from any English translation. Not that the modern English translations are wrong, it is just that we cannot find a word in English to express first-century thought.

For instance, the words "touch with the feeling" is just one small word in the Aramaic, *chasha*. That rendering comes close, but it is more than a touch; I would call it an embrace of pain or suffering. This is more than just feeling empathy; Jesus is actually experiencing your suffering and pain. He is not the kind gent who sits at your bed saying: "There, there, buck up old boy, pip pip and all that." When you suffer a broken heart, he just doesn't pat you on the head and offer the usual audibles like "Time heals all wounds, brighten up, all will be well." He actually feels your heartbreak.

Many years ago I worked for a well-known evangelist, I was often called to be in the prayer line. I have to admit I did not really appreciate this part of my job. I was supposed to pray for people as they came to the altar, and of course, most came for prayer for healing. That one got me; what if I prayed and they weren't healed. Would they get me for breach of promise? I wondered what type of liability insurance the evangelist had, and was I covered?

Well, my worst fears came to the altar after one service. It was a young man who said he had cancer and wanted me to pray that he be healed. As I quickly began to formulate a prayer, I was suddenly stricken with the realization that all I cared about was praying a nice prayer to impress this young man who could very well be dying. I had to admit to myself that I really did not care that much about this young man. I was young and healthy. How could I relate to his fears, his pain? How could I really pray that fervent righteous prayer that availed much when I felt no empathy?

So, I prayed, "Lord, I feel very little for this young man. I don't know him, I never met him before tonight, and I will likely never see him again. On top of that, I suspect that lack of empathy does not make me much of a righteous man, so how can I work up a fervent prayer. Almost, instantly there was a pain in my back that literally took my breath away. It was a pain like I had never felt before. The young man gave me a puzzled look and asked: "What's going on?" I asked him if the cancer was located in the area where I was holding my back. He sort of brightened and said: "Yes, it is." I then said: "I'm ready to pray." After praying, my pain left. I didn't ask the man if he felt anything. I just felt relief for myself and told him: "Buck up, old boy, pip, pip, and all that." He didn't hear me, he had his own little thing going on, and I left him to it.

I did learn one thing, Hebrews 4:15 needs a better rendering because God is more than touched with feeling for our infirmities. He embraces them, experiences them, and shares them with us.

I really don't remember if I did this or not, but I think I made a mental note that one day I would really search out the heart of God. I probably put it off as I was afraid of what I might find. However, 13 years ago, I began my search for the heart of God, and I found many rooms in His heart. Some are joyful, some are expectant, some are filled with celebration. I call one room His shower room where there is only one faucet that pours out the love of God, and you can stay under that shower as long as you wish.

But there are other rooms. Would you dare to enter these rooms? If you wish to pray fervently, you should consider them. I call one the weeping room. When I enter that room, I weep with God over the suffering of the world. But there is another room. It is for those of us who honestly admit that we do not feel much empathy for someone who asks for prayer. I call that the suffering room where, when you enter, you will suffer the pain and heartbreak that God feels. I believe it was that room I entered when I prayed a very fervent prayer.

THE THRONE OF GRACE – KURSIA TIVOTA

Hebrew 4:16: *"Let us therefore come boldly unto the throne of grace, that we may obtain mercy, and find grace to help in time of need."*

So, what is this throne of grace? I used to hear this verse quoted throughout my childhood on Christian radio as the station would have a time of prayer. They would begin by quoting this verse, saying, "Let us come boldly onto the throne of grace." I would then picture in my mind boldly entering this throne room and Jesus sitting on this magnificent throne surrounded by dozens of attending angels, marching right up to Him and presenting my requests.

As I grew older, I began to learn that Jesus dwells within us and that our bodies are the Temple of God. So, if there is a throne room, it is in our bodies. Then again, I find no mention of a throne in the Temple.

I went to the Aramaic, which was Paul's native language, and I found that the word throne is *kursia,* which is really a seat of honor. It is used for the chairs that a bride and groom sit in when they are lifted up by the celebrants during the wedding reception. The Talmud teaches that the guests are to form a circle around the bride and groom and dance. At some point during this dancing, they are placed in chairs and lifted up. It is believed that this is because men and women did not dance together in a wedding but form a separate group called a *mechitzah*. At some point, the bride and groom are placed in a *kursia* or chair and lifted up so they can peer over the barrier between the men and women and see each other. The couple could connect with each other by holding either end of a handkerchief over the *mechitzah*. This was a very bold move for the bride and groom to connect with each other in public. It breaks traditional protocols allowing the bride and groom to make a connection during the celebration before they are allowed to enter the bridal chamber and consummate their marriage. Despite not being proper protocol, it is accepted because they are married after all, and the whole thing takes place while everyone is dancing, rejoicing, and having fun.

This may be what Paul is talking about in coming boldly before the throne of grace. We are allowed to break traditional protocols as the bride of Christ to connect with Jesus, the groom. I believe what Paul was trying to say is that to approach the throne of grace, it is not really a somber moment but a time of rejoicing, celebrating, and dancing as one is being given grace to become the bride of Christ.

The Talmud in Avoda Zara 3b talks about two metaphorical thrones that God sits upon in relation to a proselyte. They are the throne of judgment and the throne of mercy and grace. A proselyte was an idol worshipper, non-Jew who forsook his idolatry and converted to become a Jew. A proselyte is considered born again, one who enters a new life forsaking his pagan beliefs. He is one who is leaving idolatry to become a follower of God. But proselytes, many times, will convert for lessor motives than a desire to follow God. It may be a woman who just wants to marry a man who happens to be Jewish, so she accepts his faith to become his bride. Just as in Christianity, many become Christians for motives not centered on following God but maybe to just escape hell or get certain benefits. Such a proselyte finds God sitting on the throne of Judgement.

However, if the proselyte is like Ruth, who only wants to be a follower of Jehovah, then that person will enter the throne of grace, not judgment. The bride of Christ will get a glimpse of her Groom and even be allowed to make a certain connection before that relationship is consummated.

The word for grace explains why protocol is allowed to be broken. You see, in the Jewish wedding, the bride and groom are married, and in just a short time, they will consummate their marriage, so why would it be so bad if they publicly connected if just to glimpse each other and connect on opposite ends of a handkerchief? When we accept the grace of Jesus Christ, we are married to Him, and it is just a short time until we leave this body and consummate our marriage to Him. So, why not in this time of celebration of receiving this grace, a time of rejoicing and dancing that we would catch a glimpse of the presence of our Savior.

The word bold in Aramaic is very interesting. It is *galya* (sounds like gala) and means to uncover to be visible. Just as during a *mechitzah* when the wedding celebrants are dancing and having fun, they will make the bride *galya,* visible to the groom, by lifting her in a *kursia*. So too, when we enter into the grace of God, we are lifted up in a *kursia* with Him, so He can uncover Himself not as a judge but as a loving bridegroom filled with passion.

You see, the word grace Aramaic is *tivota* which is a word used among the Semitic people in ancient times, and even today when one is granted entrance into a family community. Bedouins are often encamped as a family, with all brothers and cousins putting up their tents in a circle. Only a blood relative had access to this encampment. If someone was not a blood relative, he could not enter. Although a good friend, one who is beloved by a member of the family, may explain why this friend deserves the same rights and privileges as a blood relative and after a certain vetting process takes place being he is accepted as a family member, but he must be considered a member of the family. Even today in the Middle East, if someone considers a friend worthy of the privileges of a blood relative, he will call that friend "My brother." That is *tivota*, grace, being granted the privileges of being a blood member of a family. We are welcomed into the family of God by the Son of God, who shed His blood for us to allow us to become a member of His family through marriage.

Let us come boldly before the throne of grace means we have been granted the privileges of being a family member of God as the bride of His Son Jesus Christ.

23

MERCY SEAT – CHUSAVA'

Hebrews 9:5: *"And over it the cherubims of glory shadowing the mercy-seat; of which we cannot now speak particularly."*

The Greek word for mercy seat is *hilasterion* and is not a word found in extra-biblical literature. It appears to be a word that Paul might have coined in the Greek to follow the Hebrew word *ha kapporet*, which comes from the root word *kaphar* which means to cover. The word *kippirim* is from the same root meaning to atone. The word also is used for cleansing, purifying, wiping something clean. *Ha kapporet* is often rendered as mercy seat, which is a rendering the Jews avoid. The word in Aramaic is *chusaya*, which also means mercy seat, payment, pardon, or remission. They all mean propitiation.

Paul speaks of Jesus being the Mercy Seat, i.e., the propitiation for our sins. The high priest would enter the Holy of Holies once a year where the Ark of the Covenant was. The cover or the top portion of the ark was the *Ha Kapporet* – propitiation where symbolically the presence of God rested. Of course, His presence was everywhere, but there was a special presence upon the *Ha Kapporet*, just as there was a special presence upon Jesus as He Himself was God incarnate and the Ha Kapporet or propitiation for our sins. The High Priest would sprinkle the blood of the sacrificed lamb on the *Ha Kapporet* as the propitiation or cleansing of sins. He would literally sprinkle it upon the presence of God. This, of course, symbolized the shedding of the blood of Jesus God in human form upon the cross, shedding His blood to pay the price for our sins.

In Exodus 25:20, we learn the *cherubim* on either side of the *ha kapporet* were facing each other while the ark was in the tabernacle. However, when the ark was placed in Solomon's Temple. II Chronicles 3:13 tells us that the *cherubims* were facing *labyith,* which our English translations render as inward. However, in the Jewish Talmud in Baba Batra 99a, we learn that that *labyith* should be rendered as walls. The cherubim did not face each other in Solomon's Temple. The sages teach that this is because it was not really God's temple but Solomon's temple. The tabernacle was built to the precise specifications of God with artisans appointed by God Himself. Solomon's Temple was not built to God's precise instructions. Solomon used bronze where he should have used gold and copper. He built the temple on the backs of slave labor and imposed heavy taxes on the people to pay for the construction rather than seeking volunteers to build the temple out of love for God.

The *cherubim* covered the *ha kapporet* with their wings. Some say it was to protect the presence of God but does God's presence need protection? Some say, and rightly so, that the *cherubim*'s role was to attend to God on His throne. Every king had attendants on either side to meet their every need, so they did not have to waste time with minute details and were able to give their kingdom full attention. But really, does God need attendants to fetch him his morning coffee and bagel? Why were the *cherubim* covering the mercy seat?

A rabbi once told me that their purpose was to show God's approval. When they covered the mercy seat, and the blood was sprinkled upon the presence of God, the *cherubim* facing the presence of God showed God's approval, satisfaction, and acceptance of the sacrifice. Hence, the temple was not built according to God's direction and was, in fact, a monument to Solomon more than to God. II Chronicles 3:13 tells us that the *Cherubim* faced *labyith*, not inward but toward the walls, not over the presence of God but away from the presence of God as God was showing His displeasure over Solomon building the temple as a monument to himself and not to God.

Today Jesus is the Mercy Seat. He is the propitiation for our sins, His blood is the covering for our sins, and when we accept Jesus as our Savior, what we are doing is accepting His gift of atonement for our sins. What direction do the *Cherubim* face? Are they facing the presence of God indicating that He is taking pleasure in our redemption, or are they facing outward, away from His presence, showing that He is providing redemption, but He is not taking pleasure in it?

How can that be? For the Jews, the whole purpose of redemption is to restore one's relationship with God. However, to the Christian or most Christians, redemption is to save us from going to hell. We seek Jesus as the propitiation for our sins for our own sake to cover our own gizzard, and the relationship is sort of secondary. So, when Jesus our Mercy Seat applies His blood for our redemption, the *Cherubim* look away, for they do not approve of our motives. However, Jesus in His mercy still redeems us.

It is sort of like the old love story where a woman marries a rich man for his money and enters a relationship for the purpose of escaping a life in poverty. Yet after some time, she falls in love with the rich man, and even if the rich man goes broke, she will stay with him because she now loves him. The rich man knows she married him for his money but once married, he does his best to woo her and win her love.

Perhaps people are scared into salvation because of the threat of hell, but when God has you in a relationship, you can bet He will do everything to woo you and win your love, and those *Cherubim* will one day turn and face God's presence, for now, our relationship with God has the right motives and is true love. Even if hell turned out to be one massive party, you would have no desire to go there. Your only desire is to be with the One you have grown to love.

24

LOVE GIFT – MOHABATA

Ephesians 2:8: *"For by grace are ye saved through faith; and that not of yourselves: [it is] the gift of God:"*

If you were raised like me in a traditional evangelical church, you would be very familiar with this verse. It clearly states that we are saved by grace and that salvation is a gift of God. The next verse clearly teaches that salvation is not of any works that we do. It is purely a gift from God.

Now, something has always stuck in my mind, and I blame Christmas and Santa Claus. Many parents tell their children, "Now behave, Santa is making a list of all the naughty and nice only the nice get a present at Christmas." Aside from this being an outright lie because the kid will get his present and most likely the one he wants no matter how much of a rascal he has been, he is being taught to thank some mythical fat man who spends the entire year checking out your Facebook account to determine if you are naughty or nice. The jolly, diametrically challenged old boy can always count on big brother or sister to rat you out. Keep in mind, Alexa is on your coffee table and is listening. It totally overlooks that those gifts come from two people who love that child, and they give that gift simply because he is their child. It is called in Aramaic a *mohabata*, not just a gift but a love gift.

Around Christmas time, I get many gifts in the mail. I get those little return address stickers which I never use since I use the internet and not snail mail. I get little pads of paper or calendars and sometimes a gift of a penny or nickel, all from total strangers whom I never met and never will, all with the expectation that I will either feel guilty or ashamed of myself if I do not return that gift with a much bigger gift to help pay the cost of sending me that gift in the first place. Of course, there will be a small percentage given to the organization that hired this gift-giving outfit.

Then there are Christmas parties of sorts from church, work, or clubs where you either picked a name from an empty McDonald's cup of someone you barely know or maybe don't even like to buy a "gift" under $10.00. Sometimes you are asked to purchase a $10.00 "gift" that you will throw into some grab bag with the expectation of getting a gift of similar value. Those are not mohabata; they are just political favors, guilt gifts, gifts of manipulation, or expectations, but most often are not gifts of love.

So, there are many types of gifts. The Greek word used here for gift is a pretty general word, *doron* from the root *didomi*, which basically means a present, gift, sacrifice, or offering. It really doesn't necessarily attach any emotional value. Ah, but the word *mohabata* is built on the Aramaic word *chav,* which means love. I discussed this word in previous chapters. This gift is a gift given in love. We could almost translate this as: *"For by grace are ye saved through faith; and that not of yourselves: [it is] the* **love** *of God:"* Of course, that doesn't really express *mohabata,* as there is the idea of a gift embedded in this word. So, our Greek word is in agreement; only the Aramaic is more specific. It is still a gift. You have your choice, you can accept this gift or not. If it was just love, then everyone is saved. But it is not just love; it is a love gift. Sometimes a gift is given because one earned it or did something for it. For instance, I am often offered a tip for my services as a bus driver. The people would not offer the tip if I did not drive the bus for them. But I get paid for doing that. They, however, want to express their appreciation for going beyond my normal duties like helping them on and off the bus, carrying their packages. But, I do that, so they don't fall and sue my employer or even me, but they are appreciative and want to show their appreciation. I do not accept tips because it is a service we provide.

Here is where Santa and I come to blows. This naughty and nice stuff teaches children to be nice to get a reward. How many Christians today who need something from God will clean up their act? They will start to attend church, be nicer to people thinking God will reward them for good behavior, and will give them the blessing they pray for.

One very clear Christmas memory I have is when I was four or five years old. My Uncle Paul came into our house with a sack over his shoulder, dressed to the nines in a red outfit with a fake beard. For some reason, when

I acknowledged him for the beloved uncle that he was, I was booed down. Then he proceeded to hand out gifts, all with tags on them with not only my name but the name of the relative who gave the gift. I acknowledge the gift from my parents. Although I had no concept of the relative value of money, I did realize they usually were giving me the best gift of all. I can't remember what the gift was, but I do remember hugging my parents and thanking them out of true gratitude. But what made the gift so special was that it was from my mother and father. Later that night, after everyone went home, I was playing with my gift, and I broke it. To this day, I remember very clearly the heartbreak I felt and the tears I shed. Not over the broken gift, I don't even remember the gift, but I do remember the feeling of a broken heart that the gift my mother and father gave me, sacrifice to give to me, to show me their love was broken. Yes, even at the age of four or five, I saw a difference between the gifts from my relatives and the ones from my parents, and I was not about to thank some mythical fat man. What made it special, however, was the giver.

Our gift of salvation is given not because we were nice or good. Not because we went to church and paid our tithe. God doesn't need our church attendance or money. This is a gift of love. It is proof that he longs and desires a relationship with us so much that he even sent his own Son to die to make it possible for us to have a relationship with Him.

Tell me, when you find you broke something in your relationship with God, do you weep over that brokenness in your relationship, or do you just feel sorry for yourself that you don't have your toy to play with anymore? Or is your heartbroken over something given to you out of love and represents your love for God, and you weep because you carelessly broke it, something that the God you love so much gave to you at such a cost and sacrifice?

25

VERY NEARLY – BAQALIL

Acts 26:28: *"Then Agrippa said to Paul, "You almost persuade me to become a Christian."*

I always loved this story of King Agrippa and how he was almost persuaded by Paul to become a Christian. Whenever my father gave the message at the rescue mission in Chicago that he helped to found, he would ask me to play on the piano an invitation hymn at the conclusion, and I would play that old hymn: "Almost Persuaded." This song was inspired by the story of King Agrippa, who said that he was almost persuaded to become a Christian.

Then one day, I heard a sermon that really blew the wind out of my sails when this preacher said that in Greek, this really meant that King Agrippa was not almost persuaded to become a Christian but that he was telling Paul; "Do you think you could persuade me to become a Christian with such a little argument." I mean, I was devasted and swore that one day I would study the Greek and figure this one out for myself.

Actually, no one has really figured it out. Different translations say King Agrippa was almost persuaded, or he was not persuaded at all by Paul's arguments. In Greek, the words are *En oligo me peitheis* with so little me do you persuade. Well, that is one way to translate it from Greek, and even then, it doesn't mean he wasn't almost persuaded. Maybe he needed more than the little that Paul gave him. Another more literal translation is: "Except for a very little I am persuaded." That could be rendered in English as "You have nearly convinced me that Christianity is true." The argument is strong from both sides. But let's check this out in the Aramaic, which reads: *baqalil madam maphim*, which could read" It is very near that you persuade me."

84

Ok, I am fudging on this translation; it could also read that King Agrippa is saying the opposite. So, what is it? Was he almost persuaded, or was he not moved at all and considered Paul's arguments very weak? There is no way to be absolutely sure from the Greek or Aramaic. So, let's look at the context and what little we know about King Agrippa. Could he have had a softened heart for God? There is something very revealing in the prior verse where Paul states: "King Agrippa, believe you the prophets? I know that you believe." Paul would never be so bold as to tell a king what he believes or not, so King Agrippa must have believed the prophets, or maybe he was just pretending to be a believer in the prophets.

Let's go a little bit into the history of the kings of Judea prior to and after Jesus walked the earth. Around 134-104 BCE, about a hundred years before Jesus was born, Judea conquered Edom and forced the Edomites to convert to Judaism. For those in my Torah Study on Saturday mornings on our Learning Channel, we learned that the Edomites were descended from Esau, the twin brother of Jacob. Over the next 100 years, the Edomites gradually integrated into the Judean nation, with some of them reaching high-ranking positions. The Edomite Antipas was appointed governor of Edom, and his son Antipater was the chief advisor to the Hasmonean dynasty, which was an Edomite dynasty that established a co-ruling government over Judea with the Seleucidans who were established by Alexander the Great and defeated by the Maccabees of Chanukah fame. However, John Hyrcanus of the Hasmonean dynasty, who was an Edomite, worked his way into becoming a high priest and managed to establish a good relationship with the Roman Empire that was extending its influence over Judea about 50 years before Jesus was born. This came after their conquest of Syria. During this time, a civil war broke out between the Jews and the Edomite Hasmonean dynasty, which was quelled by Rome. Julius Caesar appointed Antipas as governor and Antipater as the chief advisor to John Hyrcanus II. Antipater was the Father of Herod the Great, who was an Edomite and convert to Judaism. Followers of Herod were called Herodians and declared Herod the Great to be the King of the Jews. This started a conflict where the Pharisees sought to restore the kingdom to the line of David where the Herodians wanted to keep the house of Herod ruling. After Herod was removed from office by the Roman government, there was a brief interval before the Herodians persuaded Rome to allow the grandson of Herod Agrippa I to be king, who was followed by King Agrippa II. His father, Agrippa I, to please the Jews, had James, the son of Zebedee, beheaded and even tried to kill Peter

(Acts 12:1-2). Tensions were rising between Rome and the Jews, and this Christian faction was not helping.

King Agrippa II was educated in Rome and was well tutored in Jewish law and traditions. He wanted to win the favor of Jewish authorities. He was Edomite by race, Jewish by faith. His grandfather Herod the Great, was hated by the Jews because of his leanings to the Roman government. There was a great division between the Sadducees who did not believe in a resurrection and wanted greater influence from the Roman government and the Pharisees who believed in the resurrection and wanted complete independence from Rome. The Pharisees were the most powerful group in Judea, but Rome was the most powerful influence.

In the seventeenth year of King Agrippa II's reign, during the reign of Nero, war was beginning to break out with Rome. Agrippa tried desperately to keep the Jews from revolting against Rome and failed. This was about the time that Paul met with King Agrippa. War broke out between Rome and the Jews, and King Agrippa sent 2,000 soldiers to aid the Roman general Vespasian and thus saving his own gizzard. He later accompanied Titus on some of his campaigns after the Jewish war of seven years between 66-73, where the Jews were forced to scatter throughout the world. The temple and Jerusalem were laid in ruins by the Romans. The Apostle Paul was executed by the Romans during the war between the Romans and the Jews. Although a Christian, he was still considered a Jew by Rome, but as a Christian, it did give Rome some pause to consider a faction of the Jews that were not nationalists. The Pharisees, of which Paul was, would make him a nationalist, which was the threat to Rome, but a Pharisee converting to this new sect might have been intriguing to Rome as a way to avert war.

Could it be that with the war pending, King Agrippa might have seen a path to a solution to the Jewish problem with Rome? Could he even consider being a Christian as a way to influence others to follow and maybe divert a war? Of maybe King Agrippa knew he was hanging onto his office by the skin of his teeth and could be assassinated at any time. Perhaps, his mind was on eternal things and making peace with God. I guess we will never know. As far as King Agrippa's heart? Was he tender to God or just politically minded? That we will never know either, one day, we will know.

26
RICH IN LOVE – DA'ATIR BARACHAMUHI

Ephesian 2:4: *"But God, who is rich in mercy, for his great love wherewith he loved us."*

If you look through the many modern English translations of this verse from the Greek you find many different renderings. The word love is repeated two times in the original text, and the word mercy is mentioned once. Yet many of our modern translations use the English word love only once. Maybe that is because it sounds redundant. The literal translation is "And God being rich in kindness (mercy) because of his great love which he loved us." It does sound a little awkward to repeat the word love even though the text thought it was important. The first use of the word love in Greek is *agape*. The second time love is used, it is *egapesen* which comes from the same root as *agape*. The word mercy is *eleei* which is a standard word for mercy in Greek; it also means compassion.

The Aramaic shows something you will not see in the Greek or the English text. For the words his great love, you have *sagia chav*. *Sagia* is an Aramaic word for great, so great it is timeless, eternal. You could render this as His eternal love wherewith he chav us. Chav, as is discussed in prior chapters, is like Ahav in Hebrew; it is the standard word for love and unconditional love.

But what He is rich in is not *chasad,* which is mercy in the Hebrew, or *chavas* which is the Aramaic word for mercy. Instead, we have the word *racham* used in an intensive form. *Racham* is always used to express God's love for us, and it is often used in Hebrew in a piel intensive form.

Aramaic Word Study

Now we learned that in Psalms 18:1, we have the only case where *racham* is used to express the love between a man and God. This is used by David, but David only uses it in the Qal, simple verbal form. He would not, could not use it in a piel form. He knew his love for God fell far short of God's love for him. Even here, it is in an imperfect form and what He is really saying is that He will *racham* or love God. He feels that He cannot achieve that *racham* love here on earth. Yet, Jesus, in John 21, asks Peter if he *rachams* him. So, at least in the New Testament, *racham* for God is achievable.

The word *racham* is a common word throughout Semitic languages, although it is used sparingly in both the Old and New Testaments. It is rooted in the word for womb. *Racham* expresses the love a mother has for the child while in the womb and the moments after it is born, and she is holding the child in her arms. She is so aware at that moment of how vulnerable the child is and how completely dependent the baby is upon her for protection, nourishment, and love. She is so aware of her responsibility for this life that is looking up at her with love and dependence she is filled with great emotion. That great emotion is *racham*. That is what God feels as He holds us, the life that He created, and when we look up to him in complete dependence for protection, nourishment, and love, he feels what that mother feels only in a piel, intensive form.

We have all heard the stories of a young mother who agrees to give her baby up for adoption because she feels she cannot care for it. Then when the child is placed in her arms, she regrets her decision and even fights to keep the child. We have all seen the grief and agony of a mother when her baby is taken away from her for whatever reason. We see it portrayed in movies, and some of us have seen it in real life. The cry, the agony, the weeping of that mother, that is *racham* a natural love and is a picture of God's love for us. We have even heard where a mother is given a choice; if the baby is born, she may die, or she can abort that baby and save her life. We have heard of mothers who will risk their lives to give birth to that baby – *racham*.

Oh, but get this, it is just *racham* in a simple Qal verbal form. It does not even come close to *racham* in a piel form. What does Paul say about this amazing love, this love that we cannot even understand? The Lord is rich in that love. In Aramaic, the word for rich is *ataira* which is a pressing toward a goal. The Lord is pressing toward a goal. The goal is to be able to fill us with His *racham* in a piel form. Picture this, God is pressing, struggling to just simply love us and become one with us in that perfect love called racham.

If God is so pressed with reaching this goal of filling us with His *racham*, then guess whose fault is it if He fails to reach that goal in us, in you?

ARMOR THAT SHINES – ZINA

Ephesians 6:11: *"Put on the whole armour of God, that ye may be able to stand against the wiles of the devil."*

Oh, the precious memories this verse brings back to me. I first heard about the armor of God in primary Vacation Bible School. Our teacher had a big picture of a Roman Warrior with all his armor, and she explained each piece of armor that was mentioned in Ephesians 6.

I mean, what child of the 50's only ten to twenty years away from World War II and a few years from the Korean war, didn't watch all those war movies on TV. We all had fathers who fought in World War II, and we loved hearing the war stories. So naturally, when our VBS teacher told of Paul's use of the warrior motif, she had our attention. During our craft time in VBS, we even made cardboard likenesses of the armor which we all wore on stage on the last day of VBS, where the chosen ones, not me, got to recite a few lines before all the parents indicating what each piece of armor represented.

We all knew what armor was for, it was to protect you, and each piece represented a spiritual asset to fight off the wiles of the devil. The word armor in Hebrew is *sharion* which means to protect, make secure. This follows the Greek word, which is *panoplian*, which means just that, armor, a complete set of armor. We do this to stand against the wiles of the devil. What are wiles? In Greek, it is *methodeia* where we get our English word method. It means to strategize, to scheme, to be crafty or deceitful. That bodes well with the Aramaic word *tseneth*, which means a plot, scheme, trick, or deceit.

Why does the enemy resort to trickery or deceit? We all know the answer to that. All he has is deceit, trickery, or lies. He was defeated at the cross when Jesus shed His blood, died, and rose again. The only way to get to us is to lie, to get us to sin, and then throw that sin up in our face when we try to worship God or seek God. He will whisper in our ear: "Just who do you think you are trying to worship such a Holy God after you committed that sin. Do you honestly think He will listen to you after all that? Really now, consider the logic."

We will scratch our head and say: "You know he's right." We will fall for his lie if we are not wearing the armor of God, which is truth, righteousness, Gospel of peace, faith, salvation, and the Word of God. We need each piece of armor not to protect us from personal attack but from lies. We just need to use our sword and quote, "The blood of Jesus has cleansed me from all my sin, you little liar you."

Note we need all the armor to stand. This word stand is the same word in the Aramaic that is used in James 4:7, where we are told to stand against the devil. This is standing for or against something. It is taking your stand. When the enemy comes, we do not retreat and hide; we are to stand against him and slash out with our sword, Word of God, if he attacks.

Well, I have not told you anything that you did not already know. I hope I reminded you, however. I mean, the enemy is wily. He will try to scare you to death, maybe even give you a vision of an ugly creature called a demon to scare you, but it is just smoke and mirrors. He can't do a blasted thing against you. If he does, he can only do it with God's permission, and you have God's covering.

Oh, but I forgot to tell you the Aramaic word for armor, my bad, it is *zina*, which means protection and security, but it also means something else, it means shiny. A good knight takes care of his armor; he polishes it every day. The very sight of a warrior approaching in shinny armor scares off the foe before he ever reaches him. Shinny armor shows the warrior is a proud warrior, brave, one who is ready for battle at all times. He never lets that polished shine fade. And when the sunlight reflects off that armor, it scares the living puddin' out of the enemy. If we don't take care of our armor, truth, righteousness, Gospel of peace, faith, salvation, and the Word of God, if we don't polish that armor every day and it loses its shine, the enemy will take advantage of it, and he will sneak in and scare you to death with his lies.

28

LAY IT ALL OUT – PERASH

Ephesians 5:10 *"Determine what pleases the Lord."*

Most of us can point to words said by someone that literally changed our lives. If I were asked what words had the greatest influence on my life, I could point to probably five occasions when someone said something that altered my life's course. One is what I heard watching the movie Chariots of Fire. The movie was about a group of men from Britain who came from different backgrounds and were preparing to run in the 1926 Olympics.

One of the main characters being portrayed was a man named Eric Liddell, who was a Christian committed to serving God. He was noted for refusing to run a race on Sunday, and rather than face elimination, he was entered into another event that he had not trained for. Yet, he still won the gold medal. His sister tried to get him to stop training and focus on this work to be a missionary. His sister actually supported his training for the Olympics in real life, but it made for good drama. To satisfy his sister, he took her to a mountain top and explained that he was going to be a missionary, but he had a lot of running to do. His explanation is what changed my life. He said: "The Lord made me for a purpose, but He also made me fast, and when I run, I feel His pleasure."

Up to that time, I considered serving God was doing religious things, read your Bible, pray, witness, testify, preach, serve in missions, etc. I never stopped to realize that there were non-religious things I could do that were just as much a service to God. Our goal is not service but to live our lives so that whatever we choose to do, we do it to please God.

If God made someone to be skilled in carpentry, then God takes pleasure in His servant building homes, renovating, or repairing. If God gave someone a "green thumb," so to speak, and the love of growing things, getting out in the hot sun gardening, and pulling weeds, God takes great pleasure in that. If God gave someone musical ability, he takes great pleasure in listening to that servant play an instrument or sing. I drove a man in my disability bus the other day. He loved God, worships God, and spent his life playing percussion instruments, like the kettle drum and triangle for the philharmonic. He played for professional musicals like the Music Man, A Funny Thing Happened on the Way to the Forum, as well as other major Broadway plays. I suppose he could have played for a Christian orchestra, but I don't think there are many Christian orchestras around, especially those in need of a kettle drummer. So, he played secular music; he did it as unto God, and he felt God's pleasure when he struck that kettle drum or triangle.

Our measure in life is not what mission board we served on, or what church we pastored, or how many we had in our church. It is measured on how well you use the gifts God has given you to bring Him pleasure.

The word in the Aramaic for pleased in our study verse is interesting. It is the word *shipira*, which means to be harmonious, to be a unifier. God gave all of us some kind of gift, and if we use that gift in His name, we are being harmonious with God and unifying ourselves with Him. But you must determine what it is that is pleasing to God. No one can tell; you can only discover that if you search your own heart. The Aramaic word determine is *perash*, which means to spread out and closely examine. What that means is that you need to spread out your life before God and examine what you are able to accomplish and what you cannot accomplish. You need to consider what you really enjoy doing because if you enjoy doing something, it is often a clue that it is something you are good at doing, although not all the time. I would like to sing. I really enjoy singing; unfortunately, nobody else enjoys my singing. But when I am alone, I will sing and make an awful noise unto the Lord, and God is pleased with my horrible sound of praise to Him. He and He alone can enjoy that terrible voice because I sing as unto Him and Him alone. If he wanted others to share the joy, He would have given me a good voice. I am good at searching words in ancient languages, and so I bring pleasure to the Lord in searching out words in the Bible, and since others seem to take pleasure in it, I share it. I used to search out words for my own enjoyment, but God has allowed me to share my findings with others, and when they say they have a new love or appreciation for God, I feel God's pleasure. It is not about making a name for yourself, having a big audience; that does not please God. What pleases God is that you perform what you were created to perform, and if you don't know what that is, Paul says to *perashm*, lay it all out and find what you are good at and what you really enjoy and do it to bring God pleasure even if He doesn't give you an audience. As long as you have that audience of one – God, you are living a purposeful life.

29
HIGH PRIEST – RABKUMRA'

Hebrews 4:15: *"For we have not an high priest which cannot be touched with the feeling of our infirmities; but was in all points tempted like as [we are, yet] without sin."*

I have often wondered why Paul pictures Jesus as a High Priest who understands our infirmities. In Judaism, the office of the High Priest ended with the destruction of the second temple in 70 AD. For us Christians, it ended with the death and resurrection of Jesus, who became our High Priest. Have you ever wondered just what that meant that Jesus is our High Priest? High Priest in the Aramaic in reference to Jesus is *rabkumra* which is translated as High Priest but is made up of the words *rab,* where we get rabbi, which means master or chief, and *kumra*, which is from the root word *kamar,* which has the idea of shrinkage or humility. The Hebrew word for High Priest is *kohan gadol*, the great or chief priest. The word in Greek is *archierea*. You may recognize the word arch and means the chief (priest).

Here is what I find interesting in the Aramaic. The Aramaic word used in the Gospels for high priest is simply *raba*, which is the word for rabbi. It does not include the word *kumra*. The role of Jesus is just not that of the High Priest but the High Priest who is humble, who has lowered Himself. You see, Jesus is the Son of God. To be a High Priest in terms of rank on a heavenly level is pretty low, lower than the angels. To be our Savior, however, He had to lower Himself to the rank of High Priest. He had to take a demotion, *kumra*, shrink down to the level of a human to assume the position of High Priest.

By why a High Priest? I did some checking in the Talmud and discovered some amazing things. For one thing, only the High Priest enters the Holy of Holies on the Day of Atonement when he offers a sacrifice for the sin of all the people. He literally takes on the sins of the entire nation as Jesus took on the sins of the entire world. But here is something you may not know that I found interesting in the Talmud Yoma 18a. The High Priest had to be rich. If he were not, it was up to the other priests to make sure he was rich. He had to be superior to everyone in his wealth, his physique, his wisdom, and his dignity. Remember *Luke 2:52*, *"And Jesus increased in wisdom and stature, and in favour with God and man."* That is exactly the requirement laid down in the Talmud for a High Priest. Although not materially wealthy, He was superior in wealth in a spiritual sense. He also had to be married and married to only one woman. If his wife were to die before the Day of Atonement, the High Priest had to remarry before he could offer the sacrifice on Yom Kippur. My study partner explained that one. Jesus as our High Priest, is married to us. For the High Priest to be married, it meant he had to share his heart with his wife and make himself vulnerable to his wife, as every man does with his wife when he gives her his heart. He gives her the ability to break his heart just as Jesus makes Himself vulnerable to us when He gives us His heart.

One other strange thing found in the Talmud in Sanhedrin 18a is that the wife of the High Priest had the right to divorce her husband, and if she did, she would be allowed to marry another man. In the Hebrew culture, only the man had the right to divorce; a woman could not get a divorce unless there were some really special circumstances. My study partner pointed out that this shows God's loyalty to us. He will never divorce us once we are married to Him. We can divorce him and marry ourselves to other Gods, but God will remain faithful to us.

There is one more thing. In the Talmud, Sanhedrin 4a, we find that a High Priest cannot be seen disrobed or naked. This would occur when washing in the *mikveh*, partial bathing, or the *tevilah* the entire immersion. This was often not a private bath but a shared bath. This was not unusual as public bathhouses were common and even exist today. Not everyone had their own private bath in those days except for the High Priest. Now here is the catcher; the High Priest could invite anyone he wants to share a bath with Him.

So, what is the parallel of this to our *Rabkumra* High Priest Jesus? Again, my study partner gave an explanation that I really like. This is again a picture of entering the heart of Jesus. Many are called few are chosen (Matthew 22:14). Many are born again, but not all are invited to share the intimacy of a *tevilah* with Jesus. That is, not everyone seeks to develop their relationship with Jesus on a daily basis in prayer and Bible Study where they become such friends with Jesus that He will trust them enough to invite them to share the intimacy of His heart. Where Jesus shares the nakedness of His heart with us reveals the deep mysteries of His heart. He is truly *Rabkumra* who makes Himself vulnerable to us. Most Christians are like the people of Israel who refused to enter the cloud. Instead, they told Moses to go in the cloud and tell them what God had to say. God's heart is available to everyone, but it is by invitation only, only to those who truly seek His heart on a daily basis, who search for Him with all their heart, soul, and might, Deuteronomy 4:29.

30

MOCKED – BAZACH

Galatians 6:7-8: *"Be not deceived; God is not mocked: for whatsoever a man soweth, that shall he also reap. (8) For he that soweth to his flesh shall of the flesh reap corruption; but he that soweth to the Spirit shall of the Spirit reap life everlasting."*

I am hearing this verse being quoted quite often these days from Christians as we face a world that is becoming more and more vocal with its anti-Christian rhetoric. Most of our modern translations say that God is not mocked. I am not sure what that means. Webster defines mockery as teasing and showing contempt in behavior or language. Some modern translations will say God will not be made a fool of. Another translation says God will not be put to shame, and still another says He will not be scoffed at. The majority of translations, however, walk in lockstep with the word mock.

The Greek word is *metrizoate* from the root *mykter*, which means nose. So, what does a nose have to do with mockery? We automatically think of thumbing one's nose, which is a sign of contempt and appears to have its origins in the 1500s during the time of Shakespeare. However, there is no record of this occurring in ancient times, particularly during the time of Paul. Still, it was such a common expression around the time of King James to flick your thumb off your nose to show contempt or mockery that translators might have assumed *mykter* indicated this gesture.

Paul could be making an allusion to *Ezekiel 8:17:* "Then he said unto me, Hast thou seen [this], O son of man? Is it a light thing to the house of Judah that they commit the abominations which they commit here? for they have filled the land with violence, and have returned to provoke me to anger: and, lo, they put *the branch to their nose."* The branch to the nose is a colloquial expression for an act of mockery and derision.

The context clearly indicates that Paul is talking of the people of God who mock God, perhaps like Judah did in Ezekiel's time. How do they mock God? They claim righteousness yet engage in abomination. Paul's native language was Aramaic, and in Aramaic, the word he uses is *bazach*, which means to mock, despise, to sneer at, and hold in contempt. It also has the idea of causing division.

Right after that, Paul warns that whatever a man sows, he reaps. It seems from the context what Paul is saying is that when you acquire knowledge of God or receive a revelation from God, don't take yourself so seriously thinking that you and you alone have the truth and everyone else is wrong, and you begin to mock those that disagree with you, especially those who try to instruct you.

We see this in many churches where the pastor gets the attitude that He is the pastor; how dare you disagree with him or suggest he might be wrong in his interpretation of a passage of scripture. After all, you are just a lowly church member under his instruction; you must show respect. You don't have a seminary and/or Bible College background. But pastors can be wrong. Teachers can be wrong. Yes, even Chaim Bentorah can be wrong. Men of God can engage in abominations and, if not checked, will result in bringing shame upon God.

But does this play out today? When the world watches us fight among ourselves, cause division, hatred among ourselves, what they see is God *bazach*, divided, they do not see a harmonious God but a God who causes division. They see pastors and men of God saying horrible things about each other why they are caught engaging in abominable acts. John Lennon wrote a song called "Imagine," where he imagined a world without religion. Why did he despise religion? He saw all the fighting, division, and hatred among religions, the hypocrisies, and abominable acts, and he desired what God desires, harmony and unity. The very place Lennon was supposed to find what he was looking for, the church, he could not find it.

That is making a mockery of God, that is bringing shame to God, that is holding God in contempt when we pursue our flesh, as Paul describes in verse 7. Our flesh desires that we are always right, that we alone have the truth, and others are wrong. It desires the things of the flesh, lust, adulterous acts, and other abominations. Our flesh demands that we elevate ourselves, and what we reap is corruption. Actually, the word in Aramaic is a bit stronger; it is *chavala'* which means binding, holding back, inflicting pain and destruction.

There are many people who no longer go to church because they have been deeply hurt by the church; they have been held back from their spiritual growth because they were not allowed to interpret the Scriptures for themselves and have felt pain over being told they were wrong and receiving condemnation for those who commit condemnable acts themselves.

During the Covid pandemic, churches were closed or had to limit attendance for almost a year due to the virus. We see a rising tide of anger and hatred toward the church. Some may say that the church has suffered from the tail of Satan, while others will say it is the finger of God. If anything, it was a time of testing for the church and a time of cleansing. Attacks against the church are continuing, and religious organizations are experiencing threats to their freedoms as never before in the history of this country. Will the church survive?

I believe the church will survive, but it will survive as a cleansed church. God will not be *bazach*. Mocked? Divided? Shamed? Made a fool of? You decided, but God will re-establish his reputation in this land with a leaner and more loving church that will reflect who He is. We will pass through the fires and the lion's den, and only the true believers will be unscorched and uneaten.

31
TRANSFORMATION – NSIONA

James 1:2-3: *"My brethren, count it all joy when ye fall into divers temptations; Knowing [this], that the trying of your faith worketh patience."*

I grew up on the KJV, and of course, as a small child, I would think as a small child. So, I would watch the adventures of Mike Nelson, a freelance scuba diver on the television series Sea Hunt and tried to watch what diver temptations he would fall into during each episode with the hope of learning what type of temptations divers experienced. Of course, eventually, I learned that the word divers was really an old English word for different. That is why I advocate the Living Bible for small children just learning to read. It is more to the language of a child. In the Living Bible, our study verse reads: "Dear brothers and sisters, when troubles of any kind come your way, consider it an opportunity for great joy." Living Bible.

I still remember the day when I was enlightened by some preacher to the fact that the word divers meant different. I think that birth the idea that I would someday be a Bible translator or study biblical languages. I would never again be fooled by the old English of the KJV. Still, that left another mystery, and that is why, when you face troubles, you should count it as all joy.

By digging a little deeper, I found that in Greek, the word for temptations was *peirasmois,* which means adversity or trials. The next verse then calls these trials *dokimion,* which is the idea of trying out or testing to determine what is genuine. In other words, all these problems we face are only to prove to you that your faith is genuine.

However, James's native language was not Greek but Aramaic, and he may not even have known Greek at all but just dictated to a scribe in Aramaic who translated it into Greek. In the Aramaic, unlike the Greek, which uses two different words for temptations and trying, there is only one word used, and that is *nsiona*, which is an amazing word because it means all that the Greek teaches and more.

In its Semitic origins, this word comes from the root word *nes*, which is used for a banner or a symbol of honor, such as a uniform worn by those who earned the right to wear that uniform. It is the same as the Hebrew word *nisayon* used in *Genesis 22:1:* "*And it came to pass after these things, that God did* **tempt** *Abraham, and said unto him, Abraham: and he said, Behold, [here] I [am].*" Our old pal KJV once again translates this *nsiayon* as tempt, but even if we put it into modern English and use the word test, that raises more questions. Why would God need to test Abraham? He knew Abraham's heart and desires. When I was a teacher, I would test my students to see how much they knew because, unlike God, I could not read their minds or hearts. But, you see, that is not the testing of *nisayon*. There is also another word in Hebrew for testing that is *bechinah*, which is a testing to show how much you know. That is the test I gave my students. *Nisayon* or *nsiona* in the Aramaic is a test not to prove how much you know but to provide an obstacle or struggle to propel a person beyond their limits.

My study partner's nephew recently completed boot camp in the Marine Corps. If you read my book Hebrew Word Study Revealing the Heart of God, he is the one who wrote that chapter on standing in the gap. He did not come back the same person he was when he left. He was more mature, more confident, and more focused. That is because the Marine Corps pushed him or *nsiona* him to his limits and then pushed him further. His family put his picture on Facebook where he was wearing his dress uniform, a uniform that only those who earn it can wear it. That is also *nsiona*, a banner or a symbol of what you are capable of doing. That uniform or *nsiona* declares to the world that he is capable of defending his country. He is capable of enduring great hardships and accomplishing things that most ordinary people cannot accomplish. He may not have counted it all joy when he was crawling through mud with a drill instructor screaming in his ear, but there was a joy in knowing if he made it through this boot camp, he would come out with another, even deeper meaning of *nsiona*, and that is the word miracle. The transformation from just a teenage kid to a man willing and able to risk his life for his teammates, his family, and his country, which to many people, for some who enter the Marine Corps it is nothing short of a miracle.

You see, you can count it all joy when you enter into many different difficulties because what *nsiona* does is to put you through the trials and difficulties that will break you down and strip you of all your trust in yourself and perform a miracle of transformation where you can raise your banner – *nsiona* for the world to see that your trust is in God alone.

32

FALL IN LOVE WITH GOD – 'EVED

Luke 4:41: *"And devils also came out of many, crying out, and saying, Thou art Christ the Son of God. And he rebuking [them] suffered them not to speak: for they knew that he was Christ."*

James 2:19-20: *"Thou believest that there is one God; thou doest well: the devils also believe, and tremble. But wilt thou know, O vain man, that faith without works is dead?"*

Someone wrote on Twitter today addressing what she believes is a controversial question; "How can our faith in God be different than the demons?"

Actually, this is the question that James himself is addressing. The demons know who Jesus is; they declared Him as the Son of God the Messiah. They believe as we do, so why are they not saved? That is why James says that faith without works is dead.

But wait one minute, does not Ephesians 2:8-9 tell us that we are saved by faith and not works? That is a very good point because the same word is used in the Greek in Ephesians 2:9 as is used in James 2:20. It is the word *ergon*, which means to work, perform a task, a deed, or action. According to the Greek, you need to back up your faith with actions. But then that means you need to do something, some work for your salvation.

The Aramaic word for work is *'eved*, which is also used in both passages, but its meaning is a little different. This is a word used for an indentured servant. In its Semitic root, according to Rabbi Samson Hirsch, a 19th Century linguist and Hebrew master, it has the idea of work that is subject to another's will. There are a lot of people who do the Lord's work, but it is not necessarily subject to the will of God. For some, it is subject to their bank account. Maybe for others, it is subject to their pride or personal identity.

Yet, even if you truly *'eved*, that is, serve according to God's will and not your own, that work will not save you. But the only way you can truly *'eved*, truly serve God for the sake of God alone and not your own, to serve no matter what the cost, no matter if it cost you your life, is to love God with all your heart, soul and might. An indentured servant will serve a master to pay off a debt or until seven years pass, and then he is free. However, he may opt to stay with his master because he has learned to love his master, and thus he can become a bondservant, one who willfully serves his master out of love and respect.

The devils believe in God and that Jesus is the Son of God, but they tremble. The word tremble is *rael*, which is a *ra'* word used for terror. The devils or demons know who Jesus is and tremble in terror. Any work they do is not *'eved*. They believe but have no love or respect for God.

If our faith does not result in love and respect for God, causing us to serve Him out of love and not personal gain, we have proven our faith is dead. The word dead in Aramaic is *muth,* which is both a physical death as well as spiritual death. Performing work or service to God without loving Him, doing it for your own benefit, that is to get answers to prayers, to be blessed, to gain heaven all for your benefit and not out of love for God then those works are spiritually dead, it has no spiritual value whatsoever.

It is the first commandment and the greatest commandment: "Thou shalt love the Lord you God with all your heart, soul, and mind." We get it backward; we seek to serve God, perform ministry, or teach Sunday School before we fall in love with God. In an ancient Jewish marriage, before a couple became physically intimate, they were first married and then spent one year betrothed. In that year, they spent much time together, but they did not share a physical intimacy until that year had passed. They did not perform the function of man and wife to produce children until they spent a year getting to know each other, share their dreams together, share their hearts, and after a year, they generally fall in love. Then they come together to produce offspring.

In Christianity, when a person gets saved, we give them a Scofield Bible, a few classes in evangelism, and send them out to make converts. God's intention is not for our first step to win the world but to fall in love with Jesus. Spend time with Him, in His Word, in prayer, and in sharing our hearts. After some time, we mature into real love, love which causes you to want to win a lost world.

The first work of faith is to fall in love with Jesus. Without that love, any work you do with your faith will have no spiritual life.

33
ANGELS UNAWARE - LO RAGASH MALAKA

Hebrews 13:2: *"Be not forgetful to entertain strangers: for thereby some have entertained angels unawares."*

For many years I have hesitated to share some of my, shall we say, supernatural experiences. However, I did release a book entitled <u>Is This Really Revival</u>? The book is no longer in print but is offered as a free download on our all Access Site. In this book, I share some rather unearthly experiences that I have kept to myself all these years, or on the rare occasion when I did share these experiences, I played them down.

Anyway, back to my book on revival, many years ago, after graduating from seminary, I was an assistant pastor in a rather liberal church that had a strong charismatic contingent. This was during the late seventies when the Jesus movement brought speaking in tongues and other manifestations of the Holy Spirit into mainstream Christianity. In Chapter 7, which I entitled: <u>The Bum</u>, I share an unusual experience. It was a very low time for me and many of the charismatics in my church. The church was on the verge of splitting, and I was about to get fired for allowing the charismatics to pray for the healing of someone with MS. The fact he was certified by his physicians as being totally free of MS only made things worse. On top of that, I was allowing the teenagers to hold nightly prayer meetings in the church sanctuary where they were yakking away in tongues. This prayer meeting was being attended by teenagers who were members of other churches, including Catholics. The was really raising eyebrows.

I was in my office with a couple of the charismatic men from the church, one was a deacon, and the other was a trustee. We were talking about how the whole situation was impossible. I felt I should resign, and they felt that they should leave the church, and we had plenty of other disparaging words. Suddenly there was a knock at the outside door and when I opened it I saw a bum. You know, your typical bum with second-hand clothes, no socks, just shoes, old newspaper hanging out of his worn second-hand sports coat pocket, matted hair, five-day-old beard, and smelling like he hadn't bathed in a month. I thought I knew all the bums in this community, it was a small town, but this old boy was a new one. I tried to direct him to the Salvation Army, but he just pointed to a grand piano near my office and asked if he could just play it for a little while. I shrugged and let him in, and went back to my office to continue our pity party. As we picked up on our conversation of woe, we suddenly heard this beautiful music coming out of that piano. The deacon asked who was playing the piano. I said: "Oh, some bum." The trustee jumped up and said: "A bum, playing the piano like that? This I have to see." I realized I had to see it also.

We went out to the piano, and the bum was playing some of the old hymns that we began to sing. We gave requests, and he knew every song we requested. The deacon and trustee began worshipping God with uplifted hands as they sang these old songs of praise and worship. I, too, in my own way, began worshipping God. Finally, the bum suggested we all join hands and pray. We did with each person praying prayers of praise and glory to God. I silently prayed and told God how much I loved Him and found myself saying, "Oh, for a thousand tongues to sing." Suddenly I was singing praise to God in words that I could not understand, but I knew I was worshipping and praising God.

After we finished, the bum quietly said goodbye and walked out the door of the church. The deacon said: "We have to stop him and take him to dinner." I ran out the door moments after he had walked out, but I could not find him. I walked around the block, but he was nowhere to be found.

I returned to my friends, who simply quoted Hebrews 13:2 and said we must have entertained an angel unaware. I know one thing, where we were discouraged and ready to quit, we were now filled with strength and determination, which led to a revival breaking out in that church.

The word *angels* in Hebrews 13:2 in Greek and Aramaic do not necessarily refer to just supernatural beings. Paul may very well be speaking of supernatural beings that appear and assist us in times of need. But he may also be referring to human angels as well. The word *angel* in Greek here is *angelous*, where we get the word *angel* from. However, it is only tradition that limits this word to supernatural beings. For instance, John the Baptist in Matthew 11:10 quotes Malachi 3:1 when he says behold I will send my messenger before thy face. The word in Greek is *angelous*, and John the Baptist refers to a human messenger. The word *angelous* is used by the Septuagint for the Hebrew word *malachi*, which means a messenger and is often used for a human messenger as well as a supernatural messenger. The Aramaic Bible, the Peshitta uses the Aramaic word *malaka*, which is identical to the Hebrew word and means both a human and supernatural messenger.

Paul is exhorting us to not be *forgetful*. In Greek, the word *forgetful* is *epilanthanesthe*, from which we get our English word *epilepsy*, and means to be *neglectful* or *forgetful*. We are encouraged not to neglect strangers. That word for strangers is not in Greek; it just uses the word *philoxenias*, which is a word for *hospitality*. However, the word *philo* is the Greek word for *friend*, and the word *xenias* is the word for *strangers*. So, we are not amiss if we render this as *do not be neglectful to show warmth and friendliness to strangers*. The Aramaic is even stronger as it is saying to not be neglectful to show *rachmetha* to *aksnaya*. *Aksnaya* is an Aramaic word used for *strangers, foreigners, pilgrims, or wanderers*. The word *rachmetha*, however, shows more than just warmth and friendliness. It comes from the root word *racham*, which expresses the idea of showing *tender mercies, deep compassion* to these wanderers that we may be entertaining. But racham, as mentioned in earlier chapters, is a God-given love. We are to love them with the love of God. They may be messengers of God, either supernatural or human. The word *entertaining* in Greek is *xenisantes*, which means *to be startled* or *be surprised*. The word unaware in Greek is *elathan*, which means to be *concealed* or *hidden*. The Aramaic uses the word *la regash*, which means to be *without rage* as well as to *be unaware*.

So, was this bum just someone sent by God to encourage us and to bring me into a newer level of my relationship with God? Was it a supernatural angel? Let me share just one footnote. I was attending a conference in a nearby town some years later, and the piano player looked very familiar. Had he been dressed like a bum, I would say... Then again, how would he have known of our need at that moment and my need to make a decision in my own relationship with God?

Again I quote as I did in chapter 1: *"There are more things in heaven and earth, Horatio, than are dreamt of in your philosophy."* Hamlet to Horatio <u>Hamlet</u> Act I Scene 5

34
GROWING CORN – QOM

James 4:7: *"Submit yourselves therefore to God. Resist the devil, and he will flee from you."*

There are few Christians who do not know this verse by memory. As to whether they know it by heart, that is debatable. What does it actually mean to resist the devil? Every modern English translation renders this as resist. Webster defines our English word resist as to withstand, strive against, oppose, to withstand the action or effect. Well, that explains it all. Do we really need to go into the original language for more? What more could there be? If we submit ourselves to God, all we have to do is oppose the devil. Maybe there is more to this than we realize.

First, let's look at the word submit. In Greek, it is *hypotagete*, which is to rank or place oneself under a specific plan or arrangement. Thus, we can only resist the devil when we place ourselves in God's plan, the center of His will. In a sense, the safest place we can be is in the center of God's will. In Aramaic, the word used for submit is *'evad*. This is a word discussed in earlier chapters. In this context, it has the idea of ownership and/or enslavement. We are to enslave ourselves to the will of God. When the enemy finds out who really owns us, he will not hang around.

But I think there is another reason he will not want to be around us. When we resist him, what are we really doing? In Greek, the word resist is *antistete* which means to set against, to withstand, to take a complete stand against, refusing to be moved. That is cool, but I don't feel that is enough to get the enemy to move.

Aramaic Word Study

Take a look at the word for devil. James uses the Aramaic word *hasatan*, which is not a proper name, but we use it anyway as Satan. Scripture does not even dignify the old buzzard with a name. The letter Hei in front of the name shows you this is not a proper name. Nonetheless, that word is not used here, at least in Greek or English. Why not Lucifer? Why not the dragon or any other name or title associated with the old goat? Why use the word devil?

The word devil in Greek is *diablo*. I bet you are familiar with that word. It means slanderous or accuser. That is exactly the meaning of the Aramaic word *hasatan* which means slanderous or accuser. So, what are we resisting? It is the enemy's accusations against us. It is his slander, accusing us of things we are and are not guilty of. He loves to slander us and fill us with false guilt.

Have you ever called upon God to help you, to protect you, heal you, or any other request, and then you hear a little voice in your head that says: "Who do you think you are? Do you honestly believe God will answer that prayer or even listen to you after what you did? Be reasonable man, you don't deserve that answer to your prayer."

You know what we do? We don't resist that thought. We play right into his little game and agree with him. What we should do is point our finger at the devil and say: "You are right, I don't deserve it, but you are also a liar, because Jesus shed His blood, died on a cross, and rose again and all those reasons why God should not answer my prayer no longer exist, they are washed away in the blood of the Lamb." We do that in the center of God's will, and the accuser will flee from us. The word flee in Greek is *pheuxetai*, which means to escape, shun or flee. But that is not the whole story. Why does he try to escape or shun us?

In Aramaic, the word used is *'eraq*, which means to be in pain and torment. He will flee from us in pain and torment. But why will he be in pain and torment from us just from *antistete* standing up to him, resisting him?

The Aramaic word used by James, the native language of James, and most likely what he was thinking about when he used this word that we translate as resist. It is the word *qom*. It means to stand against something like the Greek word antistete, but its Semitic root tells us much more. It is used for growing maize. It is a sort of corn that the people of Egypt and in the Mesopotamian area used to feed their livestock. We call it Indian corn. Almost

50% of the crops in the Middle East during the first century were maize. It was easy enough to grow because there was a lot of sunlight, and maize needed sun, a lot of sun to resist the pestilences that would attack it. It will not grow in the shade or in the shadows, well it may, but it will not be as strong.

You see, just resisting the accusations of the devil will not cause him to flee in pain and torment. We must be in the center of God's will, and we must stand in the light of God. That is what the devil hates, God's light, and he knows that the blood of Jesus is what gives us the benefit of that light. With sin in our lives, we cannot endure the light of God just like the enemy, and the enemy has us right where he wants us. But if we are cleansed, washed clean of all our sins, the light of God will shine upon us, and it will cause the enemy pain and torment. The devil was once the light bearer, and he lost that position; it now belongs to us, that is why he hates us so. For now, he cannot even stand to be in the light of God, so he will flee in torment and pain when God cast his Light upon him through us, His Light bearers.

35

LAWYERS – SAPHRA

Luke 11:52: *"Woe unto you, lawyers! for ye have taken away the key of knowledge: ye entered not in yourselves and them that were entering in ye hindered."*

Some translations say: "Woe to you experts in law," others say "law scholars" or "teachers in law." The word in Greek is *nomikois* which is one who is an expert in the law. In the Aramaic, the word is *saphra*, where we get the word scribe. The Scribes were the lawyers of their day. The Pharisees learned from the scribes. It is the scribes who knew how to read and write. Not all Pharisees knew how to read or write. Thus, the interpretation of Scripture came mainly from the scribes who knew their advantage. They knew how to read where others didn't, so if you did not know how to read, you would never dare to contradict a scribe's interpretation because there would be no way for you to disprove a scribe's interpretation.

Unlike *nomikois*, *saphra* not only referred to a scribe but to anyone who was literate and able to read and write. Thus, someone like Paul, who was not really a scribe but he knew how to read and write, was a *saphra*, and until Jesus shined a light on him, we all know how messed up his theology was.

The lesson here is that just because someone portrays himself as a Bible scholar does not mean he is accurate in his interpretation. I confess I have pulled my Ph.D. card a number of times to win an argument. If the people in the discussion group do not have a Ph.D. and do not spend 40 years studying biblical languages every day for a minimum of three to four hours, they will usually acquiesce to my argument. I am telling you my dirty little secret only because I am not the only one doing this. In fact, just let Toto pull back that curtain for a moment, and you will see that this great Hebrew Wizard is really just a friendly old man holding his kingdom together with a lot of bluff and bluster. Just like the scribe has the advantage over others because he was literate, I have an advantage because I'm literate in biblical languages. Only someone else who has studied the biblical languages would dare call me out, and if they do, it's fighting to see who has a better grasp of the language.

Once someone tells me of personal insight, if I say, "Well, that is not quite right because in the Hebrew...." Did I just take away what Jesus calls the key of knowledge for this person? The word key here in Aramaic is *qalida*, which means to lock up, to make something disappear. Jesus said that these *saphras* had the ability to make knowledge disappear by simply saying, "I can read Scripture and you can't Na Na Na Na." Yet God has a way of revealing Himself to people, and the Holy Spirit will guide them to the truth despite their so-called lack of biblical skills. But someone, a pastor, a teacher, Christian leader, or even Chaim Bentorah who has studied in a Bible College and/or Seminary intimidates someone who has no background other than being self-taught and causes them to bow to this *saphra*, then they will assume the knowledge they received from the Holy Spirit is wrong.

This is what Jesus is condemning. God can reveal His Scriptures and knowledge without the help of people with their fancy degrees and titles. Thank you very much. I conduct a Bible Study on Saturday mornings, and as far as I know, none of the participants have a Bible School background. Yet, I am amazed at the wisdom that is shared. I even share their ideas with others (based upon the fact that they likely share mine).

Jesus further states to the scribes that *"you withhold knowledge that you have not even entered into yourselves."* That means talking about something you know nothing about. Alexander Pope said, "A little learning is a dangerous thing." I have heard Christians who claim to have studied Hebrew say that the word Elohim is plural, and thus in Genesis 1:1, where God is plural, it is addressing the Godhead, The Trinity. Such a statement shows their knowledge of grammatical rules is sorely lacking. Worse, by using their "look how smart I am" card, they will hinder someone who has no knowledge of biblical languages from entering into a personal revelation that God wants to reveal to them. They have to fact-check God with a human snake oil salesman.

Jesus said one final thing: *"...and them that were entering in ye hindered."* What Jesus was telling the *saphars,* He is also telling you and me. If you have an academic background or certain credentials, you can prevent people from entering knowledge that you have not even searched out yourself just by flashing a certificate saying you finished a Hebrew course. Jesus is reminding all of us that all true knowledge comes from God, not from Chaim Bentorah or you.

36

LIVING WATERS – MIA CHI

John 4:10: *"Jesus answered and said unto her, If thou knew the gift of God, and who it is that is saying to you, 'Give me a drink;' you would have asked Him and He would have given you living water."*

Genesis 26:19: *"And Isaac's servants digged in the valley and found there a well of springing water."*

The word for living in the Aramaic and springing in the Hebrew is the same word, chi'im, which is the word for life. There is a double meaning in this. Living waters mean waters that are flowing or moving like spring water. My father grew up in the country is an actual log cabin. There was no indoor plumbing and not even a well. They met their water needs by locating a spring. He said they always looked for water that was moving, especially flowing over rocks, as they knew that was pure water.

We don't understand our dependence upon water in our culture because water is right at the tap. We are never thirsty for water, and we forget how life-giving water is. Doctors warn, especially us seniors, that we must beware of dehydration. As you get older, you do not always feel thirsty when your bodies need water, but if you don't stay hydrated, you could die. People in the Mesopotamian area in ancient times understood very well the need for water and how the lack thereof could be fatal. Thus the word chi'im became associated with spring water. Moving, flowing spring water was known as life-giving and sustaining water.

Living waters became an idiom to the ancient Hebrews for the revelation of knowledge from Torah (Rabbi Eliezer Shore). Every Jew in Jesus' day, as well as the Samaritans, knew this association or Hebrew idiom. The Samaritans, in particular, knew this because Jacob's well in Genesis 26:19 was located in Samaria. In fact, there was a certain woman who made daily use of this well. She also would have known the story behind the well. The story, which was very well known to the Jews and the Samaritans, told how Abraham dug the well and then it was sealed up with earth (dirt) or impurities by the Philistines (Genesis 26:15). Isaac re-dug the well, and again it was sealed over. Finally, Jacob unsealed the well and gave it to Joseph. The sages taught this was a representation of the revelation of Torah, which is sealed up by the impurities of the earth. These impurities or earthly passions keep one from understanding and experiencing the revelations of God.

Note how in John 4:10, Jesus is taking a very rabbinic approach to talking with the woman at the well. As a rabbinical form of teaching, Jesus was leading this woman to self-discovery by saying: "If you knew." The word knew is *yada'* in Aramaic, which means an intimacy. "If you were intimate with the gift of God and with who it is (God) that is saying: "Give me to drink...."

This may seem like a situation where Jesus is talking about something spiritual, and the woman at the well was missing the point entirely. That is not true. He was very straightforward with her, and she was responding as any good student would to a rabbi. The impropriety wasn't so much that Jesus was speaking to a woman. He spoke to women all the time, like the woman with the issue of blood, the woman seeking healing for her daughter, to Mary and Martha, etc. What was unusual was that He was engaging a woman in the form of midrash or Bible study, which could only be done with her husband. This is why it was appropriate for Jesus to ask her to call her husband before he continued with any further teaching.

When Jesus said "living water," the woman at the well instantly knew what Jesus was talking about. As a good student, she picked up on a natural illustration to discuss a spiritual issue. Her response could very well have meant: "What do you have that is so special that you can remove the impure shells that keep us from getting this living water. Are you greater than Jacob, who removed the impure shells for this well?" Jesus' response was intense. You drink of the water of Jacob, you will thirst again. In other words, "You listen to the teaching of your fathers, and you will always go to them for more. On another level, you keep seeking fulfillment in relationships, and when you find a husband who was not a *ba'al*, an abusive husband, you are still not satisfied; you still thirst again for more in that relationship. "But the water

I will give you will be in you a "well" of living water springing up into the everlasting life." This "living water" or revelation of God will not come from the teachings of your fathers but from within you, and it will lead to eternal life. "Eternal life" to the Jewish and Samaritan mind was not heaven but was that state of peace and oneness with God. What this woman was trying to fulfill in her earthly relationships could only have fulfillment in peace and oneness with God.

This is what I am trying to accomplish with Chaim Bentorah Ministries. Not to reject the teachings of your church but to expand on those teachings through a deeper study of the Word of God, to drink from the Living Waters yourself. I am reaching out to those who have attended church for years and listened to hundreds of sermons and teachings. You have become bored but are afraid to admit it, for you feel it is a sign of lack in your spiritual life. What it is, is a hunger for a Word from God. You have matured to the point where the milk of the Word is not enough, you long for more, but you can only get that from the Holy Spirit. Chaim Bentorah Ministries wants to teach you to search Scripture using the tools of the Greek, Hebrew, and Aramaic. We have dedicated ourselves to give you the tools so you can dig your own well into the Living Waters.

37

CAST OUT – NEPHAQ

John 6:37: *"All that the Father giveth me shall come to me; and him that cometh to me I will in no wise cast out."*

Casting out sounds so harsh and scary. I sure do not want to be cast out by God. So, it is a real comfort to know that God will "in no wise cast (me) out." The word for cast out in Greek is *ekballo* which means to cast out or drive out. Some modern translations say *ekballo* means that God will never reject those who come to Him. Other translations say He will not throw them out. Some are a little more gentle and say that word *ekballo* means will not you turn away. But many keep the harshness and say something to the effect that He will not drive them out.

Most translations, however, walk in lockstep with the KJV and say God will not cast them out like you toss out the trash. The Aramaic, which reflects the language of Jesus, says God will not *nephaq*, which carries the same idea as the Greek, but its usages tend to be more definitive. I have found in extra-biblical literature that it is used to describe a king who has officially left the palace even before he leaves. In other words, *nephaq* carries the idea that the very thought or rumor of being cast out means you are cast out.

Now that is why I love studying the New Testament Aramaic. God's love and caring of God are much more expressed. If we come to God, He will only not cast us out, but the very idea of casting us out will not even cross His mind. He has no plans on casting us out if we come to Him.

I had a man ride my disability bus not too long ago who told me the doctor told him to get his affairs in order for there was nothing more medical science could do for him. He already had five heart attacks, and the next one would be the big one, and it could happen any time and definitely within the next two months, more than likely within the month. He shared his life story with me as a championship bodybuilder and martial arts expert. He was the personal bodyguard for a couple of the top mobsters in Chicago and moonlighted as a bouncer in a bar. He admitted to having beaten men to death while the police looked away. He said, "I know where I am going, and I deserve to go there. The things I have done were horrible things, terrible things." I asked him to just come to God, and he said: "God wants nothing to do with me." I shared some Scripture with him and said Jesus promised that whoever came to Him He would never cast out. In fact, He would not even entertain the thought of rejecting Him. Jesus said everyone, and He meant everyone. In Aramaic, Jesus used the word *min*, which means everyone, no exceptions, no matter how horrible, how terrible the things you did, they were all nailed to the cross, and Jesus was executed for those sins, so you do not need to be punished. All you have to do is come to Him. That word come in Aramaic is *etha*, which means to simply reach out. I told him, "Don't tell me about the horrible things you did, tell Jesus and tell Him you are sorry, reach out to Him and tell Him. He promised to not reject you.

When he got on my bus for his return ride, he had a big smile and said: "I did what you suggested; I'm not afraid anymore." God will in no way toss you out if you come to Him in true repentance.

38
PREACHING IN THE WILDERNESS - MAKARAZ BACHURABA

Matthew 3:1: *"In those days came John the Baptist, preaching in the wilderness of Judaea,"*

I don't know about you, but when I see the word wilderness, I think of desert and uninhabitable land other than the creatures that wander through the desert. So, for whatever reason, I am picturing John the Baptist preaching to wild animals and bushes. The word wilderness is *eremo* in Greek, which means a place where there is no man or uninhabited, desolate, waste abandoned, and/or a desert. Yet it says he was preaching. Preaching to whom? In Greek, the word for preaching is *kerysson*, which means to proclaim, to speak publicly with conviction and authority.

In the Aramaic, the word for preaching is *makaraz* from the root word *karaz*, which means to preach or to announce or proclaim. However, it comes from a Semitic root found in both the Akkadian and Sumerian and is used for a measuring container. When a preacher preaches, he is filling the congregation with the Word of God and then measuring that congregation according to the Word of God that filled them. Is the preacher giving too much or too little? Has the preacher carefully measure the Word of God that he is filling his congregation. Sometimes a preacher can fill his congregation with too much, causing them to overreact, or too little, causing them to give little response. I believe John the Baptist was not so much preaching, as we understand preaching, but he was carefully measuring the Word of God that the Spirit of God was filling him with.

So, did John the Baptist actually do any real preaching in the wilderness? The word for wilderness in Aramaic is *bachuraba*, from the root word *charav*, which is the word for a plowed field, a field that will yield a harvest.

Actually, the Talmud has numerous references to the wilderness or plowed fields of Judaea. In Baba Kama 79b, Jews were encouraged to bring their cattle up to the wilderness or plowed fields of Judaea. In fact, the Shir Hashirim Rabbah (Song of Songs Rabbah) indicates that there were at least five cities in the wilderness of Judaea that he might have been preaching at, but I believe the word for preaching, *karaz* would indicate something more. This is likely a metaphor that he was preaching in a land ripe for harvest. He could have come into Jerusalem with a reputation as a mighty prophet of God from his preaching in the cities of the Wilderness of Judaea, but the Rabbah goes on to say that this is the wilderness where the law was revealed, the tabernacle was built, the priesthood lived, the office of the Levites was established here, and all good gifts which God gave to Israel was from the wilderness or plowed fields of Judaea.

I believe this was more a training ground for John the Baptist, and it wasn't so much the miraculous work that preceded John the Baptist that gave him credibility when he came to Jerusalem; it was the fact that he spent time in this wilderness where all good gifts from God were believed to have come. Maybe he wasn't so much preaching in the wilderness but was *karaz* in its true sense, being filled, that is, being filled with the Spirit of God in the wilderness, and any proclamations or preaching he did was worshipping and praising God as he was learning to live a life in the Spirit of God. If that is the case, poor John the Baptist spent thirty years preparing for just a few months of preaching before he was martyred.

Maybe there is a lesson in that for us. For many of us, we may spend a lifetime preparing for a ministry that could only last a few months. Yet, those few months could yield far more results than a few months of preparation and a lifetime of ministry. I was reading about astronauts who spend practically their whole lives preparing for just a few days in outer space. An Olympic athlete will spend years training, sacrificing, living in constant stress pushing his or her body its limit for just a few minutes in an athletic event. Soldiers will spend years, months, and hours just to prepare for a few minutes of combat. It is not unusual to spend far more time in preparation for an event than the time spent performing for that event.

Perhaps God has called you to spend years in preparation of Bible study, prayer, fasting, maturing for just a short ministry that will bring about eternal results.

39

VIPERS –'AKIDNA'

Matthew 3:7: *"But when he saw many of the Pharisees and Sadducees come to his baptism, he said unto them, O generation of vipers.*

Let's look further into this John the Baptist fellow. Poor John is so misunderstood. He is often portrayed as a wild, maniacal, doomsday prophet dressed in ill-fitted clothes, subsisting on bugs and robbing a bee's nest of wild honey. He comes into town looking like a wild man. Mothers hide their children, and local residents run in terror.

Let me give you a different picture of John the Baptist. Let's start with his clothing. It was not the clothing of a carelessly dressed crazy man. It was carefully chosen to convey a message. Clothing made of camel's hair was the skin of the animal with the course, itchy, stingy, thorny hair of the camel removed. He was showing his rebellion against the corrupt governmental and religious leaders who made their fortunes off the back of the common people causing them to live in poverty and suffering as if they were living in clothing covered with camel's hair. He ate locust and honey not because he was a wild man but because it was kosher (Leviticus 11:21-23) and to show he followed religious law. There is a small bird in the desert that flock together in such swarms that Bedouins call them locust and they are a food source for desert dwellers as they are easily caught. Alternatively, perhaps that is what John ate.

John the Baptist entered a town not as a mad man but as a champion of the people. As people would gather around to hear the revolutionary message of this radical out to free them from the tyranny of those oppressing them, they would see that leather girdle or belt. Suddenly their hero takes on a whole new meaning, for that leather belt is a symbol not seen for many, many years in the land of Israel. Mothers would tell their children of the days long past of men who entered towns wearing a leather belt, men who spoke from the heart of God, who prophesied of a coming day when justice would be meted out, and the faithful to God would enter a new golden age. That leather belt was the symbol of a true prophet of God.

John's message was a simple one. In the Aramaic, it is the word *tuwu*, which simply means to turn or return. In other words, if you have left your first love, your love for God, then return to it. If you have never loved God, then turn to Him and learn of His love. If you were baptized by John, it was simply a declaration that you were committing your life to love the YHWH Elohim, Lord God, with all your heart, soul, and might.

When John was baptizing, there were some Pharisees and Sadducees who attended the event. Pharisees were members of a religious order, as a Jesuit and Franciscan in the Catholic Church, some are priests, and some are laymen, but all have committed their lives in a particular service to

Many Pharisees and Sadducees stood around and listened to John. Not all were bad; they firmly believed they were helping mankind, and they were doing a lot of good. But there was a corrupt element causing many to give a sweeping consensus that all were bad.

It is these Pharisees and Sadducees that John called a generation or children of vipers. The word *viper* in the Aramaic is *akidneh*, which is really a reference to a *scorpion*. When a male scorpion mates, it quickly dies, and when the young scorpion is born, it tears the body of the mother so that the mother dies. As a result, a baby scorpion is born into this world as an orphan without the guidance of a set of parents. **John was simply declaring that the Pharisees and Sadducees were orphans. Your parent Abraham died giving you birth, and you have long lost his guidance. However, your real parent is YHWH Elohim, the Lord God.** Your salvation is not based upon your relationship with Abraham but with the YHWH Elohim, the Lord God. John's message was simply one word: "*Tuwu.*" Turn or return to your loving parent YHWH Elohim, and you will no longer be orphans without any guidance.

40

MALEFACTOR – 'AVAD BISHA

Luke 23:32, 39-43: *"And there were also two other, malefactors, led with him to be put to death. And one of the malefactors which were hanged railed on him, saying, If thou be Christ, save thyself and us. But the other answering rebuked him, saying, Dost not thou fear God, seeing thou art in the same condemnation? (41) And we indeed justly; for we receive the due reward of our deeds: but this man hath done nothing amiss. And he said unto Jesus, Lord, remember me when thou comest into thy kingdom. And Jesus said unto him, Verily I say unto thee, To day shalt thou be with me in paradise."*

I have heard people say you must be baptized to be saved; others talk about living a good life. Baptists insist you must say a sinner's prayer to get saved, which includes saying you are sorry for your sins. I do not believe any of this is biblical, and the proof lies with this malefactor on the cross who never asked Jesus to forgive his sins, was never baptized, and never had the chance to rack up some good deeds, nor was he given last rights. All he said was: "Give me heaven," and poof, he got it.

Let's take a look at this conversion experience. First, was the guy really a thief? It says he was a malefactor. Webster defines a malefactor as one who does harm or evil against another person and/or one who violates the law. No modern translation I read says he was a thief. They either call him a malefactor, criminal, or evildoer. The Greek word is *kakourgoi*, which means a criminal or evildoer, a malefactor. The Aramaic, however, uses the words *'avad bisha'*. *'Avad* is the word for a servant; it comes from the Akkadian as a word for a slave. The word *bisha* is the word for evil or wicked. This was not just a runaway slave; this is one who did something wicked to his master, possibly did him violence. Roman law had the eye for an eye philosophy, so it is very likely he and his companion murdered their master. This *'avad bisha* even admits that he did something that was worthy of death.

This is the first clue; he owns up to his sin. He doesn't even try to justify it. That right there is a true act of repentance. Without repentance, there is no remission of sin. Dr. Ben Carson, the renowned neurosurgeon, said that every event in our lives is still recorded in our brain, it is just not at the level of our consciousness, but it is there nonetheless. That means that every sin we have committed is still recorded in our brains. The Bible tells us we are to confess our sins I John 1:9. How can we confess our sins if they are no longer in our consciousness? Well, they are somewhere in our brain, and our spirits know every one of them. When we ask Jesus to forgive us of our sins, we would have just hit the button to that computer in our brain that opens up the file for all our sins that are presented to our spirit. Our spirit hits the send button and sends every one of those sins, past, present, and future, to Jesus, who then hits the delete button and erases them from his and our database; they are gone, wiped clean by the blood of Jesus.

I said future sins as well. So, does that mean we can now sin all we want, knowing we are already forgiven? Yes. But if you were truly repentant, you would not want to commit those sins; you will be so grateful to Jesus for dying for those sins you will not want to insult His sacrifice by taking advantage of it to please your own lust. In fact, you will so fall in love with Jesus that sinning is the last thing you will want to do. You will, of course, still sin, but you will also feel pretty bad about it, so bad you will not want to practice that sin. If you do, then I would question the sincerity of your commitment to God.

That malefactor could very well have been a murderer who did not have the benefit of a good preacher to warn him about hell and scare him into repentance. He did not have the four spiritual laws to guide him down the Roman Road and pray a sinner's prayer. He did not have a church full of people praying for his salvation. He had no theology to help him understand the Trinity. All he had was the Holy Spirit and some rumor that this man being executed with him claimed to be the Son of God, and unlike so many others, he believed He was, confessed it to Jesus and admitted he was a sinner and just asked to be remembered when Jesus went to paradise. Just simple faith.

41
THE COCK CROWS – QARA' TARANAGALA'

Matthew 26:34, *"Jesus said unto him, Verily I say unto thee, That this night, before the cock crow, thou shalt deny me thrice."*

Ever wonder about a rooster crowing? Why does he crow in the morning or at dawn? Why does he crow at all? According to the National Geographic magazine, a rooster feeds in the morning. He has an internal clock that alerts him to the dawn. Scientists found that if you keep a rooster in a darkened place, he will still crow at dawn, indicating that it is not the light that causes him to crow but some internal clock. Roosters do not all crow at the same time. Scientists again believe that there is a social rank among roosters. According to the Takashi Yoshimura of the Nagoya University: "Crowing is a warning signal advertising territorial claims. Our preliminary data suggest that the highest-ranked rooster has priority in breaking the dawn, and the lower (ranking) roosters are patient enough to wait and follow the highest-ranked rooster each morning."

The Talmud teaches that the third hour is the hour of the rooster's crow. The sixth hour is the time of the crow of the second rooster. Mark 14:72 says that before the cock crows twice. In the Greek and the Aramaic there is no article before the word *cock* suggesting two different birds crowing. Thus, between 3:00 AM to 6:00 AM, Peter denied Christ three times. What this suggests is that this denial was not made in the heat of passion, a weak moment when he just gave off a knee-jerk reaction. This was done over a three-hour period indicating that it was pre-meditative. Peter had three hours to think over his actions, and he repeated the denial three times.

Aramaic Word Study

The word deny in Greek is *aparnese*, which means to *look back* or to *reject* or *forsake*. Peter was not just *denying* he knew Jesus; he was *rejecting* Him. The word in the Aramaic is *kaphar* which is to *refuse* or *renounce*. It comes from a Persian word for a cyprus flower known as an alhenna by the Arabs. It is a bush or shrub that has fragrant white flowers growing in clusters like grapes. Women will dry these flowers and mesh them into a powder that they would apply as makeup to their faces to cover blemishes. The word *kaphar* is identical in Hebrew and is used for the word *atonement* which is a covering for our sins. In fact, in Hebrew, the word literally means a covering.

I believe a better understanding of what Peter did was to cover up his relationship with Jesus. In that, I believe Jesus was making a little play on words here with Peter when he said that Peter would deny or cover up his so-called blemish (his relationship with Jesus) three times where Jesus would perform three acts for atonement or cover-up for Peter's sin (His death, resurrection, and ascension to declare to the Father that the penalty for his sin is paid).

So, what could have driven Peter to reject Jesus, the Jesus that he dearly loved and devoted his life to. Was his own skin that important to him? Perhaps. Perhaps he could not believe that Jesus would allow Himself to be taken into captivity. Surely Jesus would have called lightning from heaven to strike his captors or even send angels to fight them off. Maybe he began to question that after three years, he was actually hoodwinked into believing Jesus was the Messiah when he was just an ordinary man like anyone else who had a lot of charisma and was able to build a large platform. Or maybe something else caused him to deny his Lord.

I was reading about an ancient Jewish belief in the Jewish commentary The Midrash Rabbah in Leviticus Rabbah 5 that when the cock crows announcing the approaching dawn of day, the power of the demons diminishes, their power being, for the most part, confined to night only. I don't think any of us will deny that nighttime can be a frightening time. All your horror stories take place at night; stories of ghosts appearing in haunted houses only appear at night. Even Dracula sleeps during the day and awakens only at night. Why are we so vulnerable at night? The Talmud teaches that when we sleep, our bodies and minds are at rest and unconscious.

Why did God create man to live just a short 120 years and then design him to waste forty of those years in an unconscious state? I think the Talmud is hitting on something here. During the day, our minds and bodies are always getting in the way with the cares of this world always pushing aside our spirits, which is that part of us that is in a direct link to God. Even when we worship in church, our minds are on what other people are thinking, wondering if they are watching us and if we are appearing spiritual enough. Our bodies are getting tired of standing for a half-hour or forty-five minutes while we endure the *I like God songs* with the same three chords droning on, off the guitars and keyboards. The mind is crying out, "I hate this music," and the body is crying out, "Ok, ok, I give up, I am ready to listen to a forty-five-minute sermon on a topic I have heard a dozen times before on the radio, TV, and podcasts. Just let me sit down and rest." All that time, your old spirit is just buried under the entire mind and body's belly-aching that it can't get in a praisealleluia edgewise. Ah, but when you are asleep, the mind and body have clunked out after all that ranting and raving. That is the moment your spirit has been waiting for. That is your spirit's time to rise up and say, "Ok, body and mind, it's my turn to rule the roost. I am in charge now, and God and I are going to get together for some intimate time together." So, your spirit joins with the Spirit of God in an intimacy that is just not possible when the body and mind are nagging you to death. That intimacy may be so deep that your mind and body cannot handle it. In fact, it is so deep that if God knows the past, present, and future, you too will see the past, present, and future, and you may not be able to handle even that. Something else, Dr. Ben Carson, the world-renowned neurosurgeon, said that if he were to touch one part of your brain with a sensor, you would recall every word of a book you read twenty years ago. Sometimes it is best not to remember things in the past and not know the future. When our spirits are joined intimately with God, we know what He knows, and He must cause us to forget it or mess it up in the symbolism of a dream lest it drives our already neurotic body and mind into insanity.

Perhaps the ancient rabbis are right, our spirit is free at night, and that is why the enemy sends his henchmen on an all-out assault during the night to keep us from having that intimate time with God. The enemy used the time between the crowing of two roosters because it was a time when Peter would be most vulnerable to his fears.

I would encourage you to try something before you go to sleep tonight. Command your spirit to praise God, fill your mind with the Word of God. Place flowers or diffuse sweet-smelling fragrances that your bodies will enjoy and not punish it with pizza and soft drinks that will keep you awake. In other words, invite the Spirit of God to join with your spirit, and you may wake up in the middle of the night singing worships songs or, if you are charismatic, speaking in tongues whichever way your spirit enjoys its time with the Spirit of God. But if you go to sleep watching a vampire or zombie movie or reading a racy book, then guess who you are inviting to your spirit's door, and that dream may turn into a nightmare.

I believe Peter was assaulted by demonic spirits that early morning when they were at their peak performance, and because Peter fell asleep rather than pray with Jesus in the garden, the wrong spirit came knocking at his door, and he *kaphar rejected* or *denied* his Lord.

42
AND YOU ARE IN ME - 'ANATHON BI

John 14:19-20: *"Yet a little while, and the world seeth me no more; but ye see me: because I live, ye shall live also. At that day ye shall know that I [am] in my Father, and ye in me, and I in you."*

Matthew 28:6: *"He is not here: for he is risen, as he said. Come, see the place where the Lord lay."*

Many of us baby boomers remember an old hymn we used to sing. We usually sang it on Easter Sunday morning when we had a sunrise service by Lake Michigan. It was usually cold, and everyone was half asleep from getting up early to catch the sunrise, and then the leader would have us sing one of the most difficult hymns to sing. It had unusually high notes, especially when we got to the part, "He lives, He lives." The seagulls usually joined in, and they did sound much better than the early morning screech that we called singing.

Aside from Easter, most of us usually do not think much of the resurrection. My mind is on the resurrection here in August because our Torah Portion study this week alludes to the resurrection of the believers. It is interesting that the hymn *He Lives* by Alfred Ackley was written during the Great Depression. As a pastor, he witnessed first-hand the sufferings during the Great Depression. He was a seminary student during the pandemic of 1914 and witnessed the suffering during that time. For Him, the resurrection was very important not only to himself but to the lives of his parishioners, and he preached on the resurrection of Jesus even if it wasn't Easter.

Out of those troubled times, he wrote:

> He Lives, He Lives
>
> Christ Jesus Lives Today
>
> He walks with me and talks with me
>
> Along life's narrow way.
>
> He lives, He lives salvation to impart
>
> You ask me how I know He lives
>
> He lives within my heart.

Many years have passed since that time, and again this nation is going through a crisis. There are riots, pandemics, political upheavals, and crises. Back in the mid 20th Century, there were riots and political upheavals. Students took over universities and forced the president of the university out. The National Guard was called out. Back then, the riots were over the Viet Nam War and Civil Rights. Again, Gospel songwriters Bill and Gloria Gaither were inspired to write the song *Because He Lives*.

> Because He lives, I can face tomorrow
>
> Because He lives, All fear is gone
>
> Because I know He holds the future
>
> And life is worth the living just because He lives.

There is a Torah Portion Study entitled: *Eikev*, which means *because*. What the Jewish sages teach us is that the word because is often preceded by the word why? Why should we trust God in times of trouble? Why does God allow riots, pandemics, unrest? Why should we put our faith in Him? The answer is simple, because He lives. Like in our nation's past, we are again facing troubled times like those that inspired Ackley and the Gaithers to write their songs on the living Jesus. Like those times, the acknowledgment that Jesus lives is a source of comfort driving away all fear.

In John 14, Jesus is speaking of his coming death, and he is warning his disciples of troubled times that were ahead. But He says that the world will not see Him, but his disciples and all those who love Him will see Him. Then he says a rather strange thing: "At that day ye shall know that I [am] in my Father, and ye in me, and I in you." The Greek uses the word in *en*, which means in, on, or with, exactly like the preposition Beth in the Aramaic. We could translate it as *with* if we desire. Then we would read this as "I [am] with my Father, and you are with me, and I with you." That would make more sense in the natural, but it would not fit the context. Note that in the prior verse, Jesus says that the world will not see him, but the disciples will. Commentators take that to mean that they will see Jesus after He is resurrected. However, there were non-believers who saw him also.

I conclude, like many translators, that this is talking about Jesus living inside the believer except Jesus says you will see Me. Have you seen Jesus lately? Actually, the word in Aramaic for see is *chaza'*, which means to recognize. Jesus is saying we will recognize Him because He lives, and if He lives, we will live. Ackley concluded his song with: "You ask me how I know He lives, He lives within my heart." If Jesus lives in your heart, you will *chasa'* recognize Him.

Maybe we don't see Jesus with physical eyes, but He lives inside of us, and during these troubled times, we need to constantly remind ourselves that He is alive and He lives within us.

Today I was very troubled, fearful and I could not study for my Torah Portion class; I was just too overwhelmed. But I had to prepare for the class anyway, so I forced myself to start studying, and I came across the discussion on the resurrection of the righteous or believers. My mind turned to the first resurrection. Yeah, even wearing my baseball cap to remind myself I am always in the presence of God, I still forget. I stopped and meditated on the words of Jesus, "I am in the Father and you are in me and I am in you." Even in the midst of all this craziness, we have the very God of the universe living inside of us. In the words of Thomas a Kemps, "Wherever you go, there you are." Where we go, God is there. I don't know about you but just meditating on the fact that God lives inside of me, all my fears suddenly vanished.

LITTLE CHILD – TELA'

Matthew 18:3: *"And said, Verily I say unto you, Except ye be converted, and become as little children, ye shall not enter into the kingdom of heaven. (4) Whosoever therefore shall humble himself as this little child, the same is greatest in the kingdom of heaven."*

As a rabbi, Jesus used many little educational tools to instruct his disciples. One tool used by rabbis through the ages was wordplays. Semitic languages use many different wordplays, which are easily overlooked. This particular wordplay is to take a word that has a similar sound and meaning from another language and make a playoff of that as we have in Matthew 18:3.

In Matthew 18:3, Jesus is saying that unless we become as little children. We cannot determine the wordplay from the Greek as it only works in a Semitic language. The word used in Greek for little children is *paidai*, which is the word for a little child or infant. Unless you become as a little child, you cannot enter the Kingdom of Heaven. We rightly think that Jesus is telling us that we must have the faith of a child. Tell a child a flying saucer landed out in the back yard, and he will go look, fully expecting to see a flying saucer. Does God expect us to have a faith so naïve? In my book Journey into Silence, some have suggested that I have a naïve faith, and indeed it does come across that way as I discovered the joy of childlike faith during my time in silence. No doubt Jesus is speaking of the faith of a child, but I believe He was speaking of something more, deeper, and richer.

Jesus spoke these words in Aramaic, and in Aramaic, you have two words that could be used for a child. The most common word is *yalad* which is a child or small infant. But you also have another word, *tabitha*, which is a play off the word in Hebrew *talitha*. In Aramaic, it means a child. But in Hebrew, a similar-sounding word *talitha* means a *wounded lamb*. Both share a similar root, *tela'*. I think Jesus choose to use *tabitha* from the root word *tela* rather than the most common word *yalad* to give a little wordplay.

In Mark 5:41, when Jesus raised the little girl from the dead, he said: *Tabitha Koum*. This is in a feminine form in the Aramaic and means little girl get up. But it closely parallels the Hebrew word *tela'* for a wounded lamb. Jesus could have said *yalad* rise up, which also means little child rise, but instead, he chose to use a word that plays off the Hebrew, and those who understood Classical Hebrew would instantly pick up on the wordplay. "Little wounded lamb, arise." Not all Jews in that day were fluent in Hebrew, but they would have picked up on this play on words.

When Jesus said: "Unless you become as a little child you cannot enter the Kingdom of Heaven," He used the Aramaic word *Tabitha* and could very well have intended a wordplay saying: "Unless you come as a wounded or sorrowful little child you cannot enter the kingdom of heaven." In other words, unless you are really sorry for your sins like a little child is sorrowful because his mother corrects him and he climbs into his mother's arms weeping and says: "Mommie, I'm sorry." he will not enter the kingdom of heaven. That is why Jesus further states that if you humble yourself as a child or wounded sorrowful child, you will be great in heaven.

Today politicians and celebrities are constantly apologizing for saying something that is construed as racist as you wonder if they are really sincere in their apology or they are just uttering the right words to keep their job. Children are forced by their parents or other authorities to say, "I am sorry." Most of the time, they say it under duress, but when a child really says he is sorry without being told to, it is genuine. That is the repentance God is looking for, not one under duress like the fear of hell. One of the sweetest things is to see a child who is truly sorry asking to be forgiven; it can melt the heart of a parent who will just want to hug the child and assure him of forgiveness. Not much different with God. If we are truly sorry for wounding or breaking God's heart, it will cause God to take you in His arms and assure you that all is forgiven and no punishment is needed for His Son took the punishment for you.

II Corinthians 7:10, "For godly sorrow worketh repentance to salvation not to be repented of: but the sorrow of the world worketh death." Trying to appear repentant and sorrowful after you've been caught doesn't cut it with most people if they suspect you are repentant because you must face the consequences. What is godly sorrow? True Godly sorrow is just that, Godly sorrow over having wounded and broken God's heart over your sins. For you see, it is the Holy Spirit who will convict you, break your heart and bring that sorrow. Without the Holy Spirit convicting you of your sin, you are no better off than a politician who declares repentance just to save his own gizzard. For unless you become a *tela'* a wounded little lamb, you cannot enter God's kingdom

44
BONDSERVANTS – 'AVADA

John 15:15: *"Henceforth I call you not servants; for the servant knoweth not what his lord doeth: but I have called you friends; for all things that I have heard of my Father I have made known unto you."*

The literal understanding is pretty clear. A little cultural background can be added to make it more clear, but you get the point. A friend is much better than a servant. A servant in the first-century Mesopotamian area were often just slaves. The word for servant here in the Aramaic is *avada,* which means servant, slave, and/or bondservant. In its Semitic root, it means human property. Slaves became slaves when a nation conquered another nation and took its citizens into slavery. Someone unable to pay his debt was often taken into slavery until he either paid off his debt or someone redeemed him. Sometimes a master would be so benevolent that the slave did not desire his freedom. In slavery with a benevolent master, he was well fed, had a roof over his head, and was protected. This was called a bondservant, one who willingly submits to the slavery class. Sometimes a disciple of a teacher is also called an *'Avada*, and the student would call his teacher – master. This is another form of servitude, but like the bondservant, it was voluntary.

Still, this servant was not a family member, and the master would not share any family secrets with an *'avada*, no matter how trusted. It probably happened, but it was a cultural violation to share family secrets with an *'avada*. However, a trusted servant might know everything about the master's business and even about the master himself if he was as personal *'avada*. He would know his master so well that it was like he could read his mind. In fact, many masters expected their servants to know what to offer while the master entertained guests without the master saying a word. The servant would watch his master very closely, never take his eye off the master. Just a simple glance of the eye, a nod, a smile, a frown, or some other form of communication was all that was needed for the servant to offer the guest more drink or food.

Jesus called his disciples and us *avada's*, and by the context, this is not really a slave relationship, but more of a student master relationship built out of love and trust. A master many times would not tell his student or apprentice everything. There was some jealousy or even competitiveness, and the master would hold back certain secrets of the trade to keep his student from becoming better than he. This may be what Jesus meant when He said He would no longer call His disciples *avada* but *philos* in Greek. *Philos* is a friend, not a lover, not on the level of one who has agape love, not a son or family member, just a friend. A step up from an *'avada* and step below a *ben* – son. Actually, if Jesus spoke Greek and said he was calling His disciples *philos*, they would probably be disappointed and hurt. A *philos* is not a family member, just a friend who has no real obligation as a family member would have. The disciples would have really been let down, maybe insulted, for they were hoping to be an actual member of God's family, a son, not a servant nor a *philos*. My point is, there is something not right here in the Greek.

However, the Aramaic makes it right. The word Jesus used in Aramaic to describe his disciples would have been not only satisfying to hear but would also overwhelm them, for He did not call them friends *ra'aha* in the Aramaic but *racham*. There is that word again, this time as a noun to describe a relationship. Jesus did not call His disciples friends; they were established on that level of the relationship. They were not just disciples who were trying to learn all they could from a master, Jesus did not call them *avada*s servants, slaves, or even bondservants, but He called them the highest possible position they could hold in a relationship, a *racham*. That is a newborn baby in the arms of the mother. A *racham* is more than an adopted child; it is the very child from the womb of the mother. The disciples were called *racham*, actual family members who came from the womb of God and, as a result, would share in secrets not shared with *avada*, *philos*, or even sons as a son could be adopted, but as the child from the very womb.

45
IT IS FINISHED – MASHELEM

Luke 23:28: *"But Jesus turning unto them said, Daughters of Jerusalem, weep not for me, but weep for yourselves, and for your children."*

John 19:30: *"When Jesus, therefore, had received the vinegar, he said, It is finished: and he bowed his head, and gave up the ghost."*

I have been researching the last moments of Jesus before his death on the cross. I am trying to show that He did not fear his impending torture or death like so many martyrs before and after Him. He faced his impending torture and death, not with fear but with compassion and love for us. He was willfully giving up his life.

To follow this train of thought leads me to believe that Jesus did not die as a result of the wounds of his beatings or the pain of the cross, but He died of a broken heart. Look at Luke 23:28, where Jesus addresses the Daughters of Jerusalem. Daughters of Jerusalem or Zion is a common phrase in the Old Testament, particularly in the Song of Solomon. In Hebrew and Aramaic, it is a colloquial expression, not really a reference to women but to the feminine aspect of women. The loving, caring, and nurturing nature of women. Men are also capable of loving, caring, and nurturing, but it is often associated with women, where men are associated with protection, provision, and discipline. Thus, Jesus was speaking to those in Jerusalem who had a tender and compassionate heart. He foresaw the coming destruction of Jerusalem just forty years after his death. It would be their children who would grow to adulthood when Jerusalem would be destroyed by the Romans.

Consider this, Jesus has been tortured, mocked, ridiculed, and was now being forced to carry a heavy cross to be crucified, and what are His thoughts? They are on those parents, those mothers who will bear children that will die a horrible death when the Romans come to conquer. Most really had no idea what He was talking about as he was speaking of an event that would be forty years into the future. Sort of like prophesying today of something that will take place in another half-century. Why would He speak of something that most people would not even know what He was talking about, and even if they did, they had no control over it and would likely not experience it themselves. I believe it could only have been a cry of the heart of Jesus. Jesus, as God, could not understand what real physical suffering was. Now for the first time, God, in the form of a human with a physical body, could actually feel what physical pain was like. Now He knew first-hand what suffering in the physical bodies that He created was really like. He was heartbroken over the physical pain that all humans and, at the moment, the people who would die horrible, painful deaths forty years in the future would suffer. In the midst of His suffering, He cared only for those who would suffer as He would.

Now He is placed on the cross, and in only six hours, he died. Jesus would have been in prime physical condition, young and healthy, particularly with all the exercise he got from walking. Some men would last for ten days on the cross. Many lasted for days even after a beating like Jesus received, yet he died only in a matter of six hours. Even Pilate, who ordered the men's legs to be broken so they would expire before sundown, was surprised to learn that Jesus was already dead and they did not need to break His legs. Hanging on the cross, a person could breathe in, but they could not exhale unless they used their legs to lift themselves to exhale. This is why they would break their legs so they would suffocate.

Why would Jesus have died so quickly? I say it was because he bore the weight of the suffering of the world. If His heart ached over the suffering of a future generation that would die a painful death, then how much would hanging on the cross, feeling the tremendous physical pain, the mental anguish of being mocked and rejected by the people He loved to weigh upon Him and knowing that those he loved have and would suffer like He was.

Finally, He said: "It is finished." This is a very curious word in the Aramaic; it is the word *mashelem*. It comes from the root word *shelem*, which is the same root word that *shalom* or peace comes from. The Mem in front of *shelem* in the Aramaic indicates a Pael infinitive. Unlike Hebrew, there is no infinitive construct or absolute in the Aramaic. However, similar to Hebrew the object may come either before or after. The object of this infinitive is *It*.

First, just what does *shelem* mean? It can mean to be finished, but generally, it has the idea in Aramaic to mean submission or complete submission. Then what is the object pronoun it? That is debatable. Logically we think it is Jesus saying He is about to die, but He was not yet dead, so why use a perfect tense? Why not say it is now almost finished? Something was completed before He expired, and it was submission. A God who could not die had voluntarily taken on a human form so He could know what death was like. He carried out his mission to the very end. He submitted to all that a human being experiences while on earth. We can never accuse God of not knowing what physical pain is like, what rejection, mocking, and persecution are like, and what death is like. He went through a complete cycle of submission in the flesh up to and including facing one's own certain death.

But why did He die so soon? Medically speaking, there is something called stress-induced cardiomyopathy, death from a broken heart. Dr. Stroud, in about 1847, introduced the idea that Jesus died of a broken heart. This has since been picked up by Protestants and written about in Christian literature. People do die of a broken heart. My parents were married for 67 years and were rarely apart from each other. They always got along and had a love relationship all those years. They slept in the same bed all their years, and only toward the end did my mother confess to me that my father was not quite up to it in bed, but they continued to hold each other every night. When my father passed away, my mother, who had some health issues but nothing that was immediately terminal, just went into a coma four months later. Her body shut down, and she passed away from what we call "old age." I call it a broken heart.

Jesus asked the Father to overwhelm Him with His love and compassion for mankind, but as He began to really experience the pain of mankind, it just broke His heart, and on the cross when He physically understood the pain and suffering of mankind, His heart could not take it.

It was not the Romans, the Jews, or His enemies that killed Jesus; it was His love for us and the pain of our sinful state that caused his heart to rupture.

46

MY TEACHER – RABBONI

John 20:11-12,16: *"But Mary stood without at the sepulcher weeping: and as she wept, she stooped down, [and looked] into the sepulcher, 12 And seeth two angels in white sitting, the one at the head, and the other at the feet, where the body of Jesus had lain. (16) Jesus saith unto her, Mary. She turned herself, and saith unto him, Rabboni; which is to say, Master."*

It seems much of Easter is focused on the death of Jesus, and his resurrection is almost like an afterthought. Even today, the symbol of Christianity is a cross, a device for killing someone. The real symbol of Christianity is the empty tomb. You don't hear this too much in the Easter story, but Sunday is the day He arose, not died. That is why Christians celebrate the Sabbath on Sunday, for that is the day of our redemption. The Old Testament Sabbath is the day Jesus rested in the tomb. Let's examine this first day of our redemption.

First, why did Mary go to the sepulcher or tomb on Sunday morning? We assume it was to complete the burial process of anointing the body with spices or oils. This seems a bit far-fetched as we are talking over 36 hours after the death, and thus it is not kosher to touch a dead body after that time. One would become ceremonially unclean to perform a religious ceremony. Generally, the answer would be that there would be a period of grace since Jesus died just before the Sabbath and they did not have time to prepare the body properly, and they could not do it on the Sabbath, so a little grace time was given to finish the burial process, which is why Mary arrived at dawn.

That is a possible explanation, but I do not find anything in the Talmud granting such grace periods, although I am not an expert on the Talmud. Besides, the whole reason for bringing the body off the cross just before the Sabbath was to allow enough time to prepare the body. They would not have entombed the body without proper burial procedures.

I believe a more accurate reason would be in the Semitic culture itself, which plays into the passages of John 20. It was an old Semitic custom to visit the graves of the dead on the third day after their passing to say a final farewell to the soul of the departed. It was believed that the soul hovered over the body for three days before departing. It was believed that many times the dead would return to life briefly on the third day for a short time until he fully realizes he is dead. This is a chance for a final farewell. Let's face it, they did not have modern medicine, and the definition of death was much different than today. They would yell into a person's ear, and if there was no response, they were dead. It would not be unusual for a person to be just in a state of unconsciousness and would awaken in a couple of days. Hence, they gave it three days to revive, which is why they were placed in an open tomb rather than covered with dirt. After three days, if they did not revive, they were considered dead, or they revived long enough to realize they were dead. Even today, there are many stories of someone who is totally unconscious, awakening for a brief period of alertness before dying.

Jesus did say he would arise after the third day, so it is likely Mary and the others went to the tomb with the hope of the last farewell according to Semitic tradition. Also, according to this tradition, they would anoint (not touch) the body with oils and then burn some incense as the body would "stinketh" after three days, and then they would wait for the soul to appear and either enter the body or in some way give a last farewell. It was believed that the soul would seek to find the ones it loved to say a last farewell. Thus, the loved ones would appear at the tomb to make it easier for the soul to find them. The disciples never really expected Him to actually get up and walk out.

So why did God allow them to follow such a pagan tradition? I mean, why did Jesus not just appear to the disciples at Galilee? I believe it was to show them something very important. Note when Mary looked into the tomb, what did she see? Two angels, one at the head and the other at the feet of where Jesus was laid. Two angels at each end of a slab of stone? What does that remind you of? Does it take a dusty old college professor to remind you of that picture? The mercy seat on the Ark of the Covenant where the blood was sprinkled in atonement for sin. You don't need me to explain the rest.

Perhaps Mary did need an explanation because her first words to Jesus were not "My Lord!" or "My God." It was *Rabboni.* Some texts say it is Hebrew, but the word Hebrew in the New Testament was often interchanged with the word Aramaic. It is really an Aramaic word for 'My Teacher." Either Mary instantly saw the connection between the empty tomb and the Ark of the Covenant, or she was asking Jesus to explain it to her. I don't know which, but one thing I am sure of, Jesus gave us a perfect teaching picture of His role in the redemption of our sins in that empty tomb.

NO PLACE FOR THEM - LITH DOKA

Luke 2:7-8: *"And she brought forth her firstborn son, and wrapped him in swaddling clothes, and laid him in a manger; because there was no room for them in the inn. And there were in the same country shepherds abiding in the field, keeping watch over their flock by night."*

Micah 4:8: *"And thou, O tower of the flock, the stronghold of the daughter of Zion, unto thee shall it come, even the first dominion; the kingdom shall come to the daughter of Jerusalem."*

Tradition teaches that there was no room in the inn for Joseph and Mary, and they had to settle for a stable, a cave, or a house where they put the baby Jesus in a feeding trough. This was to show His humble birth.

Well, I have been doing some reading in the Talmud, particularly in the Baba Kamma 80a and 7a,b. Here we learn that the fields of Eder, which is just a few feet bordering Bethlehem, are where the sacrificial lambs were raised and cared for. The shepherds of these lambs were elite shepherds all from the priestly tribe of Levi, whose job was to care for these lambs so they would remain without blemish or spot. They watched these sheep 24 hours a day. From the birth of a lamb, the shepherds spoiled them rotten. They wrapped them in fine linen to remain without blemish and spot, and the lambs were fed a special diet.

So, what does this have to do with the inn, which had no room available? The Aramaic text does not even mention an Inn; it just simply says *lith doka* - there was no place for them. Inns in those days were not what we think. They were little way places that were built in a circle or square and had two stories. The bottom was for the camels, donkeys, or other livestock which had feeder troughs. The second floor was where the traveler's slept. In the center was a well, and there were a number of campfires around that people shared. It was very communal and dangerous. There were no innkeepers to keep order. You might wake up and find your camels or donkeys gone, stolen. However, you stood a better chance of waking up in the morning with your livestock and supplies (as well as your life) if you stayed in one of these inns than if you did what tradition teaches Mary and Joseph supposedly did, and that was to sleep in a stable or cave which served as a feeding area for livestock.

Which, by the way, mangers and feeding locations were not very common in this area as the sheep or cattle usually just grazed and found water at various watering holes. A manger would only be found in a place like Eder, where the sheep were pampered and given a very strict diet as they were the sacrificial lambs. In fact, the only place where you would find a trough is in the Migdel Eder, that is, the Tower of Flocks. This is where the lambs which were to be used for the Temple Sacrifice would be taken for inspection and preparation to be transported to the temple.

Now there were shepherds abiding in the same country. In Aramaic, that word is *'athra* which means region, place, location. It could be miles or just a few feet away.

Many Bible scholars believe Micah 4:8 is predicting where the birth of the Messiah would take place. The Talmud predicts that the Messiah would be born in a castle. That really depends on how you translate the Aramaic word for castle. It is the word *migdel*, which could also mean a tower or a place of height or high honor. Dubious as it may seem, it was a place of high honor for the lambs, for only the best, purest, and cleanest lambs without blemish or spot were carefully examined and chosen in the *Migdel Eder* or the Tower of the Flock.

I would say that this was a fitting place for the Messiah to be born and a good reason why he was not born in a so-called inn. He should be born in the place where the sacrificial lambs are born, raised, and eventually chosen as the sacrifice.

After all, how would Mary and Joseph find cloth to make swaddling clothes, and where would they find a manger free of lice and fleas? The sacrificial lambs at the Migdel Eder were provided such clean wrappings and bug-free mangers. It would stand to reason why the angels appeared to the shepherds if you consider these were shepherds for the sacrificial lambs and were looking for the Messiah and were familiar with Oral Tradition, which taught the Messiah would be born at midnight.

My guess is that Jesus was not born in a stable, cave, or house but in a place of honor in the Tower of Miguel.

48
EATING AND DRINKING – 'ECHOL VASHATA'

Matthew 24:37: *"But as the days of Noe [were], so shall also the coming of the Son of man be. For as in the days that were before the flood they were eating and drinking, marrying and giving in marriage, until the day that Noe entered into the ark."*

I remember as a child hearing my Baptist preachers talk about how terrible the world was and how soon the coming of Jesus would be. They often quoted this verse and said: "Today it is just like in Noah's day, people are eating, drinking and giving in marriage, the return of the Lord is close." I could not help but wonder: "Didn't people always eat, drink and get married? And why is that so bad?" Well, obviously, I was just a child of little brain, and my preachers were smart enough to understand this, at least I thought they were. What they likely meant was that people were busy going about their lives such that they never expected there would be an abrupt end to everything.

However, when looking at this in the Aramaic, I wonder if maybe Jesus was giving an even deeper picture of life before the flood. In Aramaic, the word for eating is *'echol* which in its Semitic root means to consume and absorb. Your body takes in that Big Mac through your mouth, and when you eat it, it transforms those tasty little ingredients into strength, power, or energy. What is in that Big Mac that does not turn to energy is, well, you can guess what happens to that. The point is that *'echol* goes beyond just eating; it is consuming something and transforming it to benefit you and eliminating what is not beneficial to you. It doesn't have to be food. It could be a leader like a boss, politician, teacher, or pastor. Someone who seeks such control over you as to benefit themselves. When you are no longer a benefit, you are eliminated. The word drinking is *shatha*,' which in its Semitic root means to flow as water flowing down your throat. But it doesn't have to apply to just drinking. It is also used for someone who just flows with the tide, so to speak. That person who doesn't make waves. That person who is told by his boss to tell the client he is at the Cubs game when in fact, you know he hates the Cubs and is, in fact, sitting in his office at that moment. But that person will lie because his boss told him to. That is a *shatha'*. We call it turning a blind eye. Putting *'echol* and *shatha* together, you could say eating and drinking or letting some strong person exert power over you for his own benefit causing you to bend your will or forget your own morals and/or integrity.

Then there is marrying and giving in marriage. What's the difference, getting married or giving in marriage? Actually, the first word in this verse that is used for marriage is *nasan*, which in Aramaic means to take. It is used when a man says: "I am taking myself a bride." Hence translators will assume it is a reference to marriage. However, *nasan* also means to abandon. Then the Aramaic has a word that is not found in the Greek. It is the word *'anatta*, which is a reference to women with no morals or who are ceremonially unclean. In other words, women with no moral values would marry and abandon both their husbands and their children. An *'anatta* is a wife and mother who has no moral values. If the mother has no moral values, what happens to the children? They grow up with no moral values.

This phrase, "giving in marriage," is a little odd in Aramaic. The word for giving is *yahav*. This is strange because the word in Aramaic for giving is *matla*. *Yahav* means both to give and to give back. It is used for both receiving and returning a burden or trouble. The word used here for husband is rarely used for a husband. The words in Aramaic for husband are *isha* and *ba'al*. *Ba'al* literally means evil and refers to a bad or abusive husband, and the word *isha* is for a good and loving husband. The word used here is *gavar* which means a mighty warrior or a great leader or person. It is also used for a murderer.

So, let's go back to the beginning, and maybe this verse is telling us that before the flood, people were not only just living their lives as if they did not anticipate a sudden ending. We might render this as: "For as in the days that were before the flood they were consuming or using relationships with each other for their own purposes and those who did not fit their agenda they eliminated. Those who did not agree but were forced to follow forgot their morals and flowed with the times. Women had no moral principles and would abandon their husbands and children to seek their own pleasures, and mighty men would use their power to bring a burden or trouble to others, until the day that Noah entered into the ark,"

So, is that what it will be like when the Lord returns? If it is, it sure sounds like what is happening today, Gulp!

49

SON OF MAN - BREH DENASHA

Matthew 8:19-20: *"And a certain scribe came, and said unto him, Master, I will follow thee whithersoever thou goest. And Jesus saith unto him, The foxes have holes, and the birds of the air [have] nests; but the Son of man hath not where to lay [his] head."*

This is really a very interesting story. A scribe comes to Jesus and offers to go wherever He goes. A Jewish scribe in that day was a member of the aristocracy whose vocation was to transcribe letters, documents, and messages for kings and merchants. Many copied religious material, including the Torah. For this scribe to say he would follow Jesus wherever he went meant he would have to leave a good job, or he was recently fired from a job and looking for employment. Most scribes, however, were freelancers and good-paying gigs were hard to come by. This man was not interested in following Jesus and His teachings; he noticed the popularity of Jesus and knew Jesus was headed for big things. Jesus would be wined and dined by the elites, given shelter in beautiful homes, and as a scribe, he would be by the Master's side 24/7 to record any teachings, nifty sayings, or quotes. Of course, to be by the Master's side so as not to miss recording any little golden nugget, he would naturally partake of the good food and shelter offered to the master. It is a good gig if you can get it. So, Jesus's response was less cryptic than it may seem. He was telling the scribe that He was not into perks. That scribe would not become the press agent for a famous TV evangelist of a megachurch. Jesus was just a poor itinerate preacher who mostly slept on the ground at night and not in or around what would pass for mansions in those days.

What really caught my interest in this story was the use of the term Son of Man. Why did He not use the personal pronoun I? "But I have no place to lay my head." Aramaic has a perfectly good pronoun. Yet, Jesus felt it necessary to identify Himself to this scribe as Son of Man using, I should add, rather poor Aramaic grammar before a scribe of all things. They were like the English teachers of their day, and it would be like saying to your High School English teacher, "Student here has to go to his next class now." Using the term of the Son of Man in the third person was sending a very clear message.

You see, in the first-century Northern dialect of Aramaic, the term *breh denasha* or Son of Man was used quite often. It should be properly translated as human being. It is often a term used to show humility. There was *bar denasha* or the son of a man or *breh denasha* child of a human being. Jesus used *breh denasha* to say: "I am just an ordinary human being; I am nobody." Of course, Jesus was not just an ordinary human being; he was Divine and not a nobody. But this term is also used in another context which is likely the case here. It also means, "You don't know me from Adam." In other words, to use the Son of Man in the third person is like saying, "You think I am just another teacher coming down the pike, that is all you really know about me. There is no chance you are going to get a free ticket to wealth because I am not one of those teachers who will suck up to the elite and rich."

Bar is the word for son, but the word used here is *breh*, which is a word for son or daughter; it is for a child. I am merely a child of *Nasha*, which is the word for a human being, male or female. So, Jesus was saying: "I am a child of a human being." This was really a true statement, and the scribe did not seek to correct him by saying, "Ah, but you are also Divine." No, the scribe was so interested in locking up a lucrative gig he really didn't care who Jesus was, only that he was popular, and with his expertise, he would surely be a valuable asset to someone like Jesus with His potential.

There are a lot of Christian entertainers who are popular in their church and told they have great talent. So, thinking they are going to make it big in the secular world, they go to Nashville and discover they are just another kid trying to make it in Nashville and end up making ends meet by working in some mailroom. So, they go back to their Gospel roots and try to make it big in Gospel music, thinking they have a much greater opportunity there, and once they are big in Christian music, they will secure a good agent and move on to make it big in the secular world (for the sake of God of course).

But you know what? These dreamers are following Jesus for the same reason as the scribe wanted to follow Jesus – it's a good gig if you can get it; lots of influential people might be a doorway to a good career. Jesus will tell them I am a *breh denasha*, I am just an ordinary human being to you who has good connections.

50

LITTLE TWIGS - CHAV

Mark 12:30-31: *"And thou shalt love the Lord thy God with all thy heart, and with all thy soul, and with all thy mind, and with all thy strength: this is the first commandment. And the second is like, namely this, Thou shalt love thy neighbor as thyself. There is none other commandment greater than these."*

There is a little play on words here that Jesus was using, a very subtle change of words. Jesus is asked what the greatest commandment is, and he answers that you should *love* the Lord God with all your heart. Jesus was quoting a verse that was quoted every day by every orthodox Jew in his morning prayer, which is Deuteronomy 6:5. In Deuteronomy 6:5, the word *love* is *ahav*. *Ahav* is pretty much your standard word for *love* in Hebrew. Then Jesus quotes Leviticus 19:18, where we are to *love* our neighbors as ourselves. Again, the Hebrew text uses the word *ahav*.

Here is the kicker, Jesus was not speaking Hebrew. He was speaking a Northern dialect of Aramaic. The Aramaic, although a sister language of the Hebrew, is still a different language. It is a more comprehensive language. Classical Hebrew has only about 7,500 words. Aramaic has many more words; hence one word in Hebrew can have a very broad range of meanings, and when you render such a word in Aramaic, you have a variety of choices. Even the Greek does not offer as many choices for *love* as the Aramaic; you are stuck with just four Greek words which can be rendered as love. In both cases, the Greek text uses the word *agape (unconditional love)* for *loving* God and *loving* your neighbor. This creates some difficulty in understanding the subtle truth that Jesus was trying to convey. In the Aramaic text, the Peshitta, the language that Jesus spoke, He uses two different words for love. Jesus was taking advantage of the broader language of Aramaic to express the ancient classical Hebrew word *ahav (love)*. Jesus did not misquote the Old Testament commandments; he only used the broader Aramaic language to give a greater depth to its meanings. I mean, this was really clever what Jesus did.

You see, the scribes were really dealing with an age-old question. If you *ahav (love)* God with all your heart, soul, and mind, then how can you have the same love *ahav* for others. Logically, you must love others less than God if you give God such priority in your love. You cannot love God and man equally. In other words, is a man to love his wife and children more than God, equally as God, or less than He loves God?

When Jesus answered their question, speaking Aramaic, I could just see the scribe's faces light up like a light bulb (or torch in those days). Jesus used two different Aramaic words, which both are equivalent to the Hebrew word *ahav* but give a better understanding of *ahav*. If you translated these Aramaic words into Hebrew, you would most likely use the single Hebrew word *ahav*. In reference to loving God with all your heart, Jesus used the word *racham,* which is to love someone as much as they love you. It is a heavenly or Godly love. This is a love that is returned and is equal to the love that is given. We are to love God as much as He loves us. That fits the Hebrew word *ahav*. In regards to loving your neighbor, Jesus used the Aramaic word *chav*, which is very similar to the Hebrew word *ahav,* except you use a Chet rather than a Hei. A little play on words that a scribe would quickly pick up on. *Chav* is spelled Chet, Beth, which is a Semitic root word found in most ancient Semitic languages. It has its origins in a stick burning in a fire. *Chav* has been used for a *stick* and/or for *kindling*. In other words, *chav* is a kindling love. Any good Boy Scout will tell you that kindling is used to start a fire.

When I was a city-bred camp director, I used to try to start a campfire with my city-bred counselors. We would pile up a bunch of thick logs, douse it with a gallon of gasoline, stand a block away while one brave volunteer tosses a torch into the pile, and then we would run for our lives. The fire would blaze beautifully until all the gasoline burned off, and then it would die out. The next summer, the camp owners gave me a nature expert, a guy who was an Eagle Scout. I gratefully assigned him the task of building our campfire. I told him where we stored the logs, gasoline, and torches, but he said, "I will lite it with one match without using any of your supplies." He took a group of campers (we called them residents) on a field trip to the forest, where they gathered a supply of little twigs and dead tree branches in increasing sizes. He then put these branches and twigs into a pile with the smallest twigs in an opening at the bottom of the pile, which he called *kindling*. With one match, he lit the small, barely noticeable twigs or his *kindling*, and as the kindling burned, it heated the branches of the next size up long enough so they would catch fire, heating up the next largest branches until you had a roaring campfire that lasted almost through the night. It all started from some little *chav (twigs, kindling)*. There was a movie released some time ago called *Catching Fire* which is a very appropriate title as it concerns one young girl *(small twig)* who, through her sacrificial love *(chav)*, starts a fire of rebellion and (spoiler alert) revolution against an oppressive government.

You see, to love God is easy because He already loves us; we just need to return that love. Ah, but to love your neighbor is not so easy. They often do not love you to begin with, and that is why Jesus uses the word *chav* and not *racham* with your neighbor. You need to love your neighbor when they do not love you. If you persist in loving your neighbor, even when they resist your love, you will be like those little twigs that keep warming up that bigger branch, even to the point where they are totally exhausted. Yet, those twigs will warm up those bigger branches to the point where they will catch fire and begin warming up larger branches. Where there is no love among your neighbors, God has called you to be the *chav*, the kindling to start a bonfire of love in your neighborhood.

In John 13:35, Jesus says that they *will know we are Christians by our love*. I have heard Christians say, "The proof that we are the true church is that we get together and love one another. "Oh, come see how much we just love each other. Why we all join hands and sing *They Will Know We Are Christians by our Love*. How we just love each other, love, love, love, love." Well, I've got news for you; Hindus, Muslims, and Buddhists get together and love each other. Even atheists get together and love each other, so what is the difference between them and Christians? The difference is that Jesus used the Aramaic word *chav*. They will know that we are Christians because we will be the kindling to start love. We will love those who do not love us even to the point like those little *twigs (chav)* where we exhaust all that we can give. In other words, we will give our lives, even for those who do not love us.

51
BIND AND LOOSEN

Isaiah 22:22: *"And the key to the house of David will I lay upon his shoulder so he shall open and none shall shut and he shall shut and none shall open."*

Matthew 16:19: *"And I will give to you the keys to the kingdom of heaven and whatsoever you bind on earth will be bound in heaven and whatsoever you loose on earth shall be loosed in heaven."*

My study partner always looks for anything - clocks, license plates, addresses, etc. that have the number 22 as a sign from God. I thought I would give it a whirl and pick a passage like 22:22 and see if I would come up with anything. Well, this is what I get for trying to copy someone else's experience with God. But it is an interesting passage and does present a little background to a familiar passage of Scripture.

I do agree that Isaiah 22:22 is Messianic; I know that, I agree 100%. I am also not a Catholic, but I do take a very Catholic interpretation of Matthew 16:19, although I do not believe the authority given to Peter by Jesus was intended to have apostolic succession. I find no Scriptural basis to believe that such powerful authority granted to Peter was meant to live beyond Peter's lifetime. It was given only to establish the church.

Eliakim was the prime minister or finance minister to King Hezekiah. God used him as a picture of the Messiah, and I believe Jesus, as a good rabbi, used this biblical picture to explain the authority He would grant to Peter. Of course, this will leads to the obvious conclusion that I reject the popular interpretation of Matthew 16:19 that Jesus is granting to us the authority to rule over demonic spirits. Although I believe we have that authority through the Blood of Jesus Christ and the power of the Holy Spirit, I do not believe it was granted here, nor do I accept the many other interpretations that seem to be coming down the pike on Matthew 16:19. As there are many interpretations of this verse, I figure I may as well jump into the fray and wave my flag in some overt fashion. So, before you pick up rocks to throw at me, let me just explain why I believe what I do and why I am walking through this minefield. My study partner has been ripping me pretty hard with this religious bondage thing, and I need to address it, at least to myself.

In Matthew 16:19, Jesus gave the keys to the kingdom to Peter and told him that whatever he binds on earth will be bound in heaven, and whatever he looses on earth will be loosed in heaven. The words *binding* in Greek is *dein*, and *loose* is *luein*. The Septuagint uses these very same words for the Hebrew words *asar* and *hitir*. My Aramaic Bible, the Peshitta, shows the Aramaic word 'esar for *bind*, which is directly related to the Hebrew word 'asar and the Aramaic word *shira* for loose, which is also directly related to the Hebrew word *hitir*. Both of these words are legal terms found throughout the Mishnah and Talmud and represent *forbidding* and *permitting*. The council of sages and rabbis of the Sanhedrin were granted the authority (by man) to *asar or 'esar (bind)* and *hitir or shira (loosen)* Jews to aspects of the law. It was believed that whatever the rabbis *bound 'asar, 'esar* on earth was *bound* in heaven, and whatever they loosened *hitir shira* on earth was loosened in heaven. This was recorded in the Tradition of the Fathers during the time of Jesus, which eventually became the Jewish Talmud. The word *heaven* was just another term used to represent God, so one would not speak the sacred name of God. Thus, it was believed that what the Sanhedrin ruled whether to *bind 'asar, 'esar,* or *loosen hitir, shira,* was automatically ratified by God. It would seem that Jesus used this same popular expression to grant similar authority to Peter to resolve future disputes in the establishment of the church.

We find one such example of this *binding 'asar, 'esar* and *loosening hitir, shira* to take place in Acts 15 where the apostles and elders convened in a sort of *Church Sanhedrin* in Jerusalem to address the issue as to whether Gentiles were bound to the law. In Acts 15:10, we find Peter exercising his *rabbinic* authority granted to him by the very lips of Jesus of *binding 'asar, 'esar* and *loosening hitir, shira* to declare that the commandments were too heavy for the Gentiles and that they should be loosened from the obligations of the law. In verse 20, James chimed in and said that he agreed but that the Gentiles should still be bound by laws that the Jews considered universal prohibitions such as murder, adultery, and idolatry, etc. In verse 22, it appears everyone gave a hearty *amen* and then sent Paul and Barnabas out to spread the Word.

From this, I believe the issue of the law and our obligation to the law was resolved and later confirmed by the Apostle Paul in the first century and under the authority of *binding 'asar, 'esar* and *loosening hitir, shira* granted to Peter by Jesus. We, as Gentiles, are not bound to the Judaic laws that are indigenous to Judaism, such as the dietary laws, laws of festivals, tithing, etc. But we are bound to those laws that are considered universal laws, such as murder, adultery, idolatry, etc. It helps to look through Jewish literature to find out what the universal laws are, but the Holy Spirit does a better job at that within our own hearts.

The point is, if you look at Isaiah 22:22 and Matthew 16:19 from a Jewish historical and cultural context, it would help us understand the significance of Acts 15 and maybe cause us to rethink our interpretation of Matthew 16:19. Also, it may help us gain some insight into our obligation to the law. Many a rabbi have told me that as a Gentile, I am not *'asar, 'esar (bound)* to the 513 commandments and *hitir, shira (loosened)* from all but the 10 commandments. Some have even said I am only bound to 3 of the 10 commandments. But I prefer to take my cues direct from the Spirit of God.

52
LET YOUR LIGHT SHINE – NANOOHAR NOOHARKVA

Matthew 5:15-16: *"Neither do men light a candle, and put it under a bushel, but on a candlestick; and it giveth light unto all that are in the house. Let your light so shine before men, that they may see your good works, and glorify your Father which is in heaven."*

Today I was feeling sorry for myself because I just do not have the opportunity to speak to live audiences. Speaking to a live audience has so many dynamics that speaking into a recording or doing a live Facebook or Zoom meeting does not have. I not only love to speak, but everyone who hears me tells me how good I am at it. Yet, here I am, just writing and doing my Facebook and Zoom thing. Over and over, I ask God why but then today, I reflected on an old song or hymn made popular around 1910 – 1920 by Billy Sunday.

Back at the turn of the 20th Century, a brilliant young woman named Ina Duley Ogdon was selected to be on the Chautauqua Circuit. This was back in the early 1900s before radio and television, and people had little opportunity to attend colleges or listen to an educated lecture. Thus, the Chautaugua Circuit was created as a traveling college, so to speak, and became an extremely prestigious lecture circuit supported by President Theodore Roosevelt himself.

Those chosen to lecture and teach would travel all over the United States, set up tents, and speakers would deliver lectures on many subjects, including Christianity. Young Ina was a gifted orator, and this was her life's dream to travel and lecture. But just before leaving, her father was injured in an accident, and she felt obligated to turn down this chance of a lifetime to remain with her father and care for him. Although she did not begrudge her duty to care for her father, she was confused as to why God gave her such an opportunity to spread his Gospel and the gift of oratory to deliver that message and then just snatch it away.

One day as she cried her heart out to God as to why she could not use her gifts in such a prestigious manner, she read Matthew 5:16: *"Let your light so shine before men that they may see your good works, and glorify your Father which is in heaven."* She suddenly realized her only duty was to let her light shine through any venue God gave her, even if only in her own community. She found peace in her calling soon wrote these words: "Here for all your talent, you may surely find a need. Here reflect the Bright and Morning Star. Ever from your humble hand, the bread of life may feed. Brighten the corner where you are."

These are the initial words to the song that she wrote: "Brighten the Corner Where You Are." Billy Sunday picked it up, and it became like his theme song, like "How Great Thou Art" became with Billy Graham.

But what does that mean to let your light shine? I remember as a child in Sunday School, we would hold up our index finger and sing: "This little light of mine, I'm gonna let it shine, shine shine." But I never really understood what that meant. For one thing, why would you hide a light in the first place? Some commentators suggest that this was the Chanukah Menorah which was kept out of sight from the Romans for fear of persecution. Maybe. More than likely, it was a reference to homes which in that day had only one room and no place to hide any valuables if someone should visit. So, they would extinguish the light and invite the guest to step outside into the sunlight or moonlight to talk if they feared this visitor was casing the joint.

The word light is in Greek in *lycnnian,* which means a physical light or lampstand. Its meaning is limited, but the metaphoric implication is clear. However, the word used in the Aramaic is *noohra* which is a word with extremely broad meanings and would have great significance to those Semitic Aramaic-speaking people listening to Jesus. *Noohra* means light, but it has many possible usages to the Semitic mind. Here are just a few usages of *Noohra* and what might have been going through the listener's mind when

Jesus said to let your light or noohra shine – teaching, enlightenment, brilliance, intelligence, the Torah, God's presence, faith, forgiveness, humility, meekness, peace, justice, love and purity of heart.

What was happening to the Jewish people of Jesus's day (and to Christians today) is that Israel's Light as is the Light of the Christians has been buried under so many commentaries and teachings beyond biblical study that their and our Light cannot shine through. Not only that, Jewish teachers and leaders, as with many Christian teachers and leaders, focused their attention on matters that so interest people that they seek to build a platform rather than build the spiritual lives of the people they teach. There were many aspiring teachers who were never chosen to be discipled by a master teacher and so figured that they would never have the chance to express the talents that God gave them as they had no real audience or platform. They did not have the right credentials like Peter, James, John, and the other disciples, so they buried their talents.

Jesus was saying to let your *noohra,* your gifts, your teaching, enlightenment, brilliance, intelligence, Torah, God's presence, faith, forgiveness, humility, meekness, peace, justice, love, and purity of heart shine in your *bita,* your house. He did not say the temple, the synagogue, the city, nation, or the world. He said, your *bita,* your house.

In other words, brighten the corner where you are. So, I have a little corner, I drive a disability bus, I write for a blog and a subscription site. I have no major platform, no great following; I have what God has given me, but He expects me to brighten or spread my *noohra* in that little corner.

53

COLD WATER – GAR

Matthew 10:42: *"And whosoever shall give to drink unto one of these little ones a cup of cold water only in the name of a disciple, verily I say unto you, he shall in no wise lose his reward."*

There were some things in the first century that have not changed in over 2,000 years. Jesus is referencing one such attitude. People are always ready to do a favor for someone who has wealth or status because they expect something in return, some reward. The word *little ones* in Greek is *mikron*. Today we use the word micro to describe something small, microscope, microbe, etc. *Mikron* means something that is little or small. So, what does it mean to give a cup of water to a small or little one? Obviously, if you are giving a cup of cold water to someone small, you are speaking of a child. Hence most translations make mikron an adjective and add the word one, i.e., little one or a child. But that is really just paraphrasing. A few translations will say one who is humble, i.e., small in self. We think of a humble person as one who does not seek to draw attention to himself.

In the Aramaic, the word that is used is *zeora*. It is where we get our English word zero. It could mean a person who is young or a child. But its use in the Talmud and Targum is often to suggest a person who has suffered some sort of setback in health or finances. It is sometimes used for an elderly person whose strength has diminished and can no longer perform the way he used to. We often hear an elderly person who has lived an active and fruitful life bemoan that they are not worth much anymore.

The word for cold water in Aramaic is *dqarura* from the root word *qar*, which simply means cold or chilled. I often hear preachers read this as a cup of water, assuming the emphasis is on water. If that were the case, the text would use the word *mayim* – water rather than *qar* – cold. The emphasis is on the word cold. When someone draws water from a well, it comes up very cool and refreshing. Often the one who draws the water will quickly take a drink of that water to take advantage of its refreshing cool taste. In the climate of the Middle East, that water quickly loses that cool, satisfying crispness. If someone approaches you as you draw up the water and asks for a drink, such as Jesus did with the woman at the well, the person drawing the water would likely take the first drink from his cup to take advantage of its ultimate coolness and then offer some to the other person once their thirst was quenched. By the time the person has satisfied his thirst, the water is no longer as cool as it was when it was first drawn, and thus, they would share the water that has lost its chill and would not be as satisfying. However, if a person of importance were to ask for a drink of water, you would not hesitate to offer him the first drink of *qar* – cold, as you want to be on his good side and possibly get some reward for offering him a cold drink of water.

Jesus was telling his disciples that if they gave a drink of cold water in the name of the disciple or in the name of the teachings of Jesus to a person of diminished reputation, strength, or health, to someone that could offer no reward, they would still get a reward. In other words, don't go out seeking the wealthy, the leaders, the politicians, the celebrities to share this message with, but treat everyone as an equal and share with whoever you have the opportunity to share.

I was in a fairly large church filled with zeoras, people of ordinary rank who struggled to even give a tithe or offering. These people had wonderful testimonies of the love of God in their lives and how God had delivered them from some real struggles. Yet, the pastor never asked them to give a word of testimony. One day the owner of the largest car dealership in town started to attend our church. Almost immediately, our pastor asked this man to come forward and give a testimony. He was quickly made a deacon and given an adult class to teach. The pastor wined and dined him and showed him off to any guest speaker or denominational leader that visited our church. The pastor made sure that everyone knew this wealthy community leader was a member of our church. In less than a year after his first visit, we never saw this man again in our church. I suspect he realized that he was just being patronized and used. The pastor was left with egg on his face trying to explain to the many who asked him: "What happened to so and so?"

54

WHEN YOU PRAY – TSALU 'ANATIN

Matthew 6:9: *"In this manner, therefore, pray: Our Father in heaven, Hallowed be Your name."* **NKJB**

Matthew 6:9: *"After this manner therefore pray ye: Our Father which art in heaven, Hallowed be thy name."* **KJV**

Some years ago, a publisher came out with the New King James Version of the Bible, assuring the brothers and sisters that they in no way changed the old King James; they just updated the archaic language like using "you" for "ye." I remember a well-known fundamentalist going on television assuring the King James people that this new edition was the true King James translation; nothing was changed except using modern English to make things clearer.

Well, take a close look at Matthew 6:9 in the NKJB and the Old KJV and tell me if you do not see a major change. At least to me, as a teacher of biblical languages, this is a major deviation, and if Christians only knew the importance of this change, the King James only people would be appalled.

Do you see it? They did not change the "pray ye" to "pray you." In fact, they left the "you" completely out of it. Let me share with you how important that little pronoun is to understanding what Jesus is trying to teach. In fact, that little word is the fundamental purpose of Jesus giving this prayer, and I did not even notice it until I was preparing for my Torah Portion class on the Sukkot, the Jewish Festival of Booths. Here I discovered the Jewish people actually follow the teachings of Jesus much closer than we do when it comes to prayer.

The word "you" in Hebrew is *atah*. In Aramaic, it is *anatin*. Both mean more than just you. It refers to a level that is the source of all Jewish souls and, for that matter, the source of all born-again Christians. It called the *Knesset Yisrael* or the Congregation of Israel. For us as Christians, it is the fellowship of believers. The word fellowship in Aramaic *shauteph* corresponds to the Hebrew word *asephah*. This is the word used in Exodus when the plague of flies came upon Egypt. Actually, the word does not really mean flies; it is assumed it was flies. It is really a word for swarming insects. You see, the ancients noticed that when the Nile overflowed and flooded the land, it washed away many crawling insects, except one, the fire ants. They are tiny creatures that would easily wash away, but when floods come, they gather together, clinging to each other to create a giant raft that floats on the water. Ancient believers noticed this and used the word *shauteph* for fellowship. Christians who swarm together for protection. When the storms come, they gather together and form a life raft to weather the deluge.

The Jews remind themselves that they are one. They practice something called the *Amidah*, the word *Amidah* means to stand, but there are a number of words in Hebrew for standing. This word is used for standing to *prepare yourself to do something*. This is a prayer to prepare yourself for prayer. Have you ever prayed to prepare yourself for prayer? The Catholic church does it all the time when they recite the "Our Father" or what we call the Lord's prayer. The *Amidah* prayer is *Barcheinu ainu kulanu k'echad*. I wrote it out in Hebrew so you would catch all those *nu's*. Those are all plurals. This translates out as "Bless us, our Father, all as one.

In the Jewish mindset, when you pray, even when you pray by yourself, in your closet, you are united with all Jews; all souls are as one. There is no *me* being angry at *you* because there is no me versus you. They are all one. This is as it should be in our Christian faith; in fact, that is why Jesus gave us the "Our Father." It is declaring our unity, our oneness as one in Jesus Christ.

Listen to what you say when you pray the "Our Father." Note it starts off as "*Our* Father." It is not "*My* Father." Even when no one is around you, pray "*Our* Father." Then it say's "Give *us* this day *our* daily bread." It does not say, "Give *me* this day *my* daily bread." Oh, then Jesus doesn't stop there. You are not only to include your brothers and sisters in the Fatherhood of God, in prayer for nourishment, but what else? "Forgive *us our* trespasses as *we* forgive those who trespass against *US*. When someone trespasses against a fellow believer, they are trespassing against you as well. Yes, even in asking forgiveness of sins, we are to include our Christian family, and we must forgive those who have sinned against our brothers and sisters, even if that sin does not affect us personally. "Do not allow *us* to fall into temptation but deliver *us* from evil." How many times do we smile when we see a brother or sister we have struggles with fall into evil?

Note Mark 11:25: *"And when ye **stand** praying, forgive, if ye have ought against any: that your Father also which is in heaven may forgive you your trespasses."* When you stand – Amidah praying. It is all about being united in the family of God.

This whole prayer that Jesus gave us was not for us to memorize and repeat in rote memory word for word. It was a model for us to follow as an example. It was to be used for "when you stand" or Amidah to prepare you for prayer.

I challenge you the next time you pray alone in your closet, drop the personal pronoun "I" and "me" and use the plural "you" and "us." See if it does add a new dimension to your prayer life.

55

AIR KISS – SEGAD

John 4:23: *"But the hour cometh, and now is, when the true worshippers shall worship the Father in spirit and in truth: for the Father seeketh such to worship him."*

I am researching for a book seeking to understand the means and ways of worship among the ancient Hebrews and then trying to find a modern context. To research this book, I am interviewing various worship leaders from different denominations and churches who have various styles of worship. I am beginning to find that many of these worship leaders were hired or given the position to lead worship because of their musical ability. To many, worship is simply the musical portion of the service. It is hard for them to imagine a worship service without music. I find few really have a biblical perspective on worship, as they seem to be just copying what they have seen other worship leaders do. I remember one worship leader who felt sorry for a fellow worship leader in another church who could not find a good drummer. It was hard to imagine that God would not bless this church with a good drummer as they sincerely wanted to worship God, but of course, without a drummer, your worship would suffer. I was going to ask if he felt such empathy for King David, who did not have the benefit of electric guitars and keyboards.

My point is this, it seems even our leaders spend little time trying to understand what worship really is. Most just tend to go with what works or what others are doing. We forget that there was a time when music was not allowed in churches, and when it was permitted, you could only sing or chant from the book of Psalms. But who am I to criticize? The woman at the well was under the impression that worship could only take place in a certain geographical location. Her worship leaders said they could only worship on a certain mountain, but others said in Jerusalem. Even in those days, people questioned what their religious leaders told them to believe, and for good reason, because Jesus pointed out how wrong they could sometimes be.

Jesus told this woman that for true worshippers, it is not a geographical location but a matter of the heart; that true worshippers worshipped in *spirit and truth*. In Greek, the word spirit is the word *pneuma*, which is the word used for the *Spirit of God, the human spirit, breath, or wind*. But this woman Jesus was speaking with did not speak Greek; she spoke Aramaic. In Aramaic, the word Jesus used was *rucha*, which is identical to the Hebrew word *ruach* and has the same meaning as the Greek *pneuma*, meaning the *spirit or the Holy Spirit or breath and wind*.

However, it is the word for *worship* that has me spooked. In Greek, it is *proskyneo*. Now watch this. This is a compound word *pros* for *throw or toward* and *kyneo* for the word *kiss*. Worship is throwing a kiss to God. Well, maybe a little cultural background is needed. In Aramaic, the word is *segad*, which comes from a loan word from the Middle Egyptian for an *air kiss*. When the Egyptians worshipped their gods, they were not allowed to touch the idol even with a kiss, so they would breathe through their nostrils onto the idol, and that was considered a kiss or an *air kiss*. Air passing through the nostrils became known as an *air kiss or a segad*. Later in Greek, it was known as a *proskyneo* which being interpreted means *to worship*.

Remember, in Genesis 2:7 God breathed into man's *nostrils* the *breath or nephesh* of life. Yet, here we are not worshipping God with our *nephesh*, but with *rucha*, which is the word used for the *Ruach Kodesh or Holy Spirit*. I found the word *rucha* is preceded by a Beth in John 4:23, which in Aramaic is the word *by*. Hence, we do not worship *in* the Holy Spirit but *by the Holy Spirit*. God breathed the *neshemah physical life* into us through the nostrils, but we breathe *His Spirit our spiritual life* out of our nostrils to Him. We worship *by the Holy Spirit*. Without the Holy Spirit, we cannot worship God. If we allow the Holy Spirit to take control of our lives, He will draw out of us our love to God. I read something interesting in Mark 9:39 this morning: *"But Jesus said, "Do not hinder him, for there is no one who will perform a miracle in My name, and be able soon afterward to speak evil of Me."* When I read this, I could not help but think of something I read in Jewish literature. It was a story of a student who complained to his rabbi that another student only studied Torah so he could show off his great knowledge and impress everyone with his understanding of Torah. The rabbi replied, "Don't hinder him, for the Torah will purify his motives."

I sort of blasted worship leaders at the beginning of this study so let me conclude by saying this. Perhaps there are worship leaders out there who are frustrated rock star wannabes or desire to show off their talents. Perhaps there are worshippers seeking to impress the others with their holiness by loud expressions of worship or performing physical contortions. Don't hinder them, for if they are expressing the name of Jesus, then let the Holy Spirit purify their motives, and they will not speak evil of our Lord. For it is only by the Holy Spirit that any of us can truly worship God in truth. In Aramaic, that word *truth is sharara. Sharar* is a word that means to be *tightly bound together.* It is like the strands of fabric tightly bound together to form a rope. *Sharar* is the word used to express that *tight bonding, a bonding so tight that nothing can break it.* When we *worship segad,* that is, give God an *air kiss breathing or sharing the life of His Spirit with Him,* we create a bond with Him that can never be broken.

Worship is *segad sharara,* that is, allowing the Holy Spirit to bond us tightly with God.

56
FAIL - NAPHAL

I Corinthians 13:8 *"Charity never faileth: but whether [there be] prophecies, they shall fail; whether [there be] tongues, they shall cease; whether [there be] knowledge, it shall vanish away."*

I am a Baptist who likes to get emotional about my relationship with God. As any good Baptist knows, you must not trust in feelings; therefore, I found myself hanging around the Charismatics because they like to feel and get all emotional about God. Although these Charismatics do have some strange ways. One I would like to address is this business of personal prophecy. You can't hang around the Charismatics very long before someone lays hands on you and starts to say words like: "The Lord wants you to know He has everything under control; you are very near you're breakthrough." Some of the more advanced prophets will say that the Lord has a great ministry for you, you will find a job that will pull you out of debt, etc. Most of the time, these prophecies are harmless, and if you buy into them, they can be of real encouragement. I, however, being raised a Baptist, was told that such personal prophecies do not exist today. I Corinthians 13:8 is the poster child of Scripture to back this up. My Baptist friends will say, "Lookie here, prophecies cease." The KJV says they will just fail, which is the usual defense.

The word used in the Greek for fail or cease, as many modern translations translate it is *katargethesontai* which comes from the root word *katargeo*, which means to bring to naught, abolish, annul, make of no effect. In the Aramaic, the word is *naphal*, which is actually a word used for an abortion. To bring a pregnancy to an end. Our English words cease and fail fit nicely into these definitions, so we really need to check other sources to determine

173

if prophecies are done away with or not. That has been done to near exhaustion, so I would just like to take another approach.

I would like to check out the Talmud and see if we can find some help there. Most Christians do not even know what the Jewish Talmud is. Many equate it with the Kabbalah and call it a mystical book which the Talmud is definitely not. The Babylonian Talmud is called Babylonian because it was compiled by Jews in Babylon and has nothing to do with Babylonian paganism. For the sake of understanding, let's just call it a Jewish commentary, which is highly inaccurate, and I know I will be hearing from a few of my Jewish friends for calling it that, but I do need to put this into terms that Christians understand. It is fifty-two volumes of centuries of comments, opinions, and musing of literally thousands of rabbis and sages. Now before you throw rocks at the Jews for studying and researching the Scriptures using the input of earthly teachers and scholars, let me throw out a few names like Augustine, Thomas Aquinas, Calvin, Wesley, Tozer, Scofield, and I can continue with more names that Christians feel are the authoritative and final word on interpretation of Scripture. We have our rabbis and sages, too and they are just as revered as the Jewish sages. I've sat through many sermons where I have heard, "Scofield says this, and Wesley says that, and of course, let's not forget the old sage, Augustine." Of course, we call Augustine a church father, not a sage, and Scofield a teacher and not a rabbi. They are just as capable of inaccuracies as the sages and rabbis in the Jewish Talmud.

Some people will say, "Why go to that Jewish literature when we have a library full of Christian teachers to learn from?" My answer to that is that I do not find that our Christian teachers have all the answers. Besides that, why not go to the source of knowledge that Christianity was birthed in, which is Judaism. The first Christians were Jews, Jesus was Jewish, the Bible is a book about the Jews. The Jews are the masters of the Hebrew language and the guardians of the Old Testament. I have found their insights and musings have cleared away a lot of the cobwebs of misunderstandings in the Bible that our Christian fathers did not or could not.

So, let me go into this study and present to you something for your consideration. Maybe there is merit to it; maybe not that is for you what you feel God is revealing to you to decide.

That Talmud in Yoma 9b and Yoma 21b tells us something very interesting. There were five things in the first temple that were not in the second.

They were the ark of the covenant, the Shekinah, the fire from heaven, and two other rather surprising things, the Holy Spirit and the Urim and the Thummim. The Talmud further teaches that after the death of the latter prophets, which would be Haggai, Zachariah, and Malachi, the Holy Spirit was removed from Israel.

The Holy Spirit would not return until the Messiah was glorified. Look at *John 7:39 "But this spake he of the Spirit, which they that believe on him should receive: for the Holy Ghost was not yet [given]; because that Jesus was not yet glorified."* What does that mean? What does it mean that Jesus was not yet glorified? According to what I have read in Jewish literature, the Messiah must suffer humiliation and pain, death, resurrection, ascension, and be established on the throne of His kingdom before the Holy Spirit will return to Israel. Jesus suffered humiliation, pain, death, resurrection, and ten days after his resurrection, he ascended to heaven. Jesus died on Passover, and fifty days after Passover is the Feast of Weeks. This is also known as Pentecost or the first fruits where the Jews celebrate the beginning of a new season with their produce and offer to God the first of their harvest as an offering. This first fruit could very well be a symbol of Jesus. This might explain why Jesus told his disciples to wait for the coming of the Holy Spirit. Forty days after his ascension to heaven was the Feast of Pentecost, where the offering of the first-fruits was accepted by God. Pentecost would have completed the glorification of Jesus and thus allowed the Holy Spirit to return. Of course, we are all familiar with what happened in Acts 2.

Note *I Corinthians 6:19: "What? know ye not that your body is the temple of the Holy Ghost [which is] in you, which ye have of God, and ye are not your own?"* Our bodies are now the temple. When the Holy Spirit who dwelled in the temple returned, He returned to the temple, our bodies. When the presence of God, which rested upon the Ark of the Covenant, returned, it returned to the temple, our bodies. When the Shekinah returned, it was to our bodies; when the fire of God, in its symbolism, returned, it was to our bodies. When the Urim and Thummim returned to the temple, it returned to....wait a minute.

What were the Urim and Thummim? These were some objects; we are not sure just what they were. The Talmud teaches it was the ephod worn by the High Priest and the stones represented not only the twelve tribes of Israel but also were used to represent the Hebrew Alphabet when they would light up. This was used by the High Priest to determine the will of God, the direction of God, or very much what my Charismatic friends say to me when they prophesy over me.

Come on, just grant the old professor his ponderings or speculation, which all that this is. I am not introducing new doctrine, dogma, or revelation, just musing like many of the old rabbis and sages, church fathers, or preachers. Could it be that my Baptist friends are right, did prophesy really cease? But in place of it, we received the Urim and Thummim. What the Urim and Thummim were meant to accomplish is now in the new temple, our bodies. What my Charismatic friends call prophesying over me is really using the Urim and Thummim that once dwelled in the temple but now dwells in all of us who are in Christ Jesus and have the Spirit of God, the fire of God and Shekinah dwelling in us along with the Urim and Thummim.

Alright, don't listen to me; I am just an eccentric old professor, but I tell you next time one of my Charismatic friends prophesies over me, I am not going to think he is a prophet, nor am I going to think prophecy. I am thinking Urim and Thummim.

ASKING IN THE FLESH

Matthew 18:19-20: *"Again I say unto you that if two of you shall agree on earth as touching anything that they shall ask it shall be done for them of my Father which is in heaven. For where two or three are gathered together in my name, there I am in their midst."*

"Where two or three are gathered together to study Torah, the Divine Presence is in their midst." **The Talmud**

The most common interpretation of Matthew 18:19-20 is such a sacred cow for Western Christians that if anyone dared suggest that our interpretation is even slightly contrary to the standard interpretation, it would be like suggesting that apple pie and mothers were un-American. Yet, every time I attend a prayer meeting, and I hear someone say, "Let's agree in prayer," I can't help but stop and think about what they are really saying. I mean, is God going to be more motivated to answer prayer if three people are praying than if one. What if I am alone and have no one to pray in agreement with me over an urgent matter? Am I out of luck? Is God up there in heaven shaking His head, saying, "Chaim, Chaim, when are you going to learn you need at least two or three others agreeing with you in prayer before you can expect an answer." Doesn't that contradict what it tells us in James 5 that the prayer of a (that is one) righteous man can avail much?

In the Greek, Matthew 18:19 literally reads: *"Again, amen, I am saying to you that if ever two shall be in agreement out of you on the land in every matter that they are requesting it shall be becoming to them."* Here is the key, the idea is not to be ganging up on the Lord and storming the palace hoping he will give in and give you want. It is the idea that someone is agreeing with you that your request is within the will of God. If that person does not agree, then a third person is called in to arbitrate the dispute and bring everyone into agreement. In James 4:3, we learn that: *"Ye ask, and receive not, because ye ask amiss, that ye may consume [it] upon your lusts."* The word amiss in Aramaic is *dabishiait*, which has the idea of asking in the flesh. In other words, you are praying for fleshly desires and not heavenly desires.

The Aramaic word Jesus used for agree is *nashatuon*, which in this particular grammatical form means to be found worthy. When people come together to pray, many have various motives. Some like to show off their piousness, some like to preach a little sermon when they pray or to show off their great oratory ability, some just pray out of group pressure. But if only two or three are praying the fervent prayer of a righteous person, and they are worthy, that is, they are not asking to fulfill their own fleshly desires or lust but only to fulfill the will of God, the request will be granted. Where two or three are found worthy, i.e., they are not asking for their own vanity but for the sake of the kingdom of God.

Jesus almost quotes in verse 20 from Oral Tradition, which later became the Talmud. The Talmud teaches: "Where two or three are gathered together to study Torah, the Divine Presence is in their midst." Ancient Jews, and even today, would never study Scripture alone. The Talmud admonishes one never to study the Torah alone. Some people would actually hire someone and pay them to study the Torah with them just so they would not have to study it alone. Of course, you are going to say that the passage in Matthew is clearly speaking about our prayer request and not studying the Bible. We would say that because our mindset in our Western Culture is "me" oriented. To many people, God is merely a celestial vending machine. Pop in a few token prayers, push the button, and out comes what you want. For many in our Western society, Christianity is a marriage of convenience with God. The purpose of such a marriage is to ensure that one's personal needs come first. In Jewish thinking, however, it is a marriage of love where the needs of the other come first. So, we approach Matthew 18 not as "Ah-ha, a formula to get my prayers answered" but rather as another deep teaching by Jesus. The reason the Talmud says, "Where two or three are gathered together..." and most likely why Jesus used this common expression of His day is that when two people study together, a problem sometimes arises. The two may disagree over how to interpret a passage. When this happens, a third person, often a rabbi, is brought in to bring the two into an agreement. It also happens when we make a request to God. We should have a prayer partner who will confirm our request. If there is a disagreement that the request is not of God but of the flesh, you may need to bring in a third party to help bring all into agreement that they are praying the will of God and not asking out of fleshly motives.

Simply put, this passage is speaking more of the unity of the body rather than offering a formula to get your prayers answered.

58
RECEIVE – QAVAL

Mark 9:37: *"Whosoever shall receive one of such children in my name, receiveth me: and whosoever shall receive me, receiveth not me, but him that sent me."*

Several years ago, I was asked to speak in a church. The church had a balcony, and during the worship service, I went to the balcony just to observe the people as they worshiped and experience their joy. I also believed God wanted me to observe the worship rather than participate as I felt He was going to show me something interesting. As I sat watching the worship, I suddenly noticed a little child, no more than three or four years old, run out to a little open area along the side of the auditorium and begin to spin around in a circle. Immediately my spirit was quickened, and I knew this was why God wanted me to observe rather than participate in the worship service.

First, I noticed that the father did not restrain his child from "playing around" during a worship service. The father was not worshipping with the rest of the fellowship, at least not like they were; he was too focused on his child as he sat away from the rest of the fellowship and just enjoyed the music and the spirit of worship while he kept his eye on his child. I really felt that God's heart was warmed by this, and as a result, this father was *receiving* God as God was *receiving this* child. I also firmly believed that this father was worshipping God through his child.

The child was really too young to understand the dynamics of worship. She was just participating in the joy that she was feeling around her. I could not help but think of various passages of Scripture at that moment, but one really stood out in my spirit. This was Mark 9:37. I realized she was worshipping God just as much as the adults standing around were worshipping God. I recalled reading in Jewish literature how children would often worship God by spinning around in a circle. In fact, we find in II Samuel 6:14 that David *danced* before the Lord in front of the Ark of the Covenant. The word in Hebrew here for *danced is chayl* which means *to spin around in a circle.* This is why David's wife had a fit over this demonstration as he was acting like a child. I often wondered why David suddenly began to *dance* or *spin around* before the Ark. Perhaps there were some children along the way spinning around, and David sensed the presence of God upon them, and he too began to spin around with them. This child may not have known she was worshipping God, nor did the father know that he too was worshipping God as he observed his child. Not only that, I found that by just observing this child basking in the joy of the Lord by spinning around in a circle, I was moved to tears like I would be if I were in a very intense and intimate moment with my God.

Is this what Jesus meant when he said: "whosoever receives one of such children in my name; receives me." In the Aramaic, the verse reads: "Whoever receives a child like this in my name receives me." Interesting that the word in Aramaic for child is *tela*, which is a word for a little lamb and sometimes for a wounded lamb. A little lamb has no sense at all. It will graze with the rest of the flock but could easily become so involved in grazing that it will not even notice if the flock has left and the little lamb is left alone. The lamb is totally incapable of finding its way back to the shepherd or the rest of the flock. All it can do is stand there and baa. Have you ever heard a little lamb baa? It sounds almost like a child crying. A little lamb is totally dependent upon its shepherd and struggles to be close to its shepherd. But earthly distractions such as eating can cause it to take its eyes off of the shepherd, and when the *tela'* little lamb looks up, the shepherd and flock are gone. Does that sound familiar? Sometimes we become so preoccupied with the things of this world that when we look up, it is as if God is no longer there. But He is, just as the shepherd is still there and will leave his ninety and nine to search for his lost lamb. Just as God will put everything aside to search for you if you are lost. You not only lost Him, but He's also lost you, and He is desperate to reunite with you.

In our study verse, the first time the word for *received* that is used in this verse has a Daleth before it indicating the word *that.* The word is also followed by the preposition Mem, which could give a rendering of: "Whoever receives from that child in my name will receive me." Hence, we could render this as: *"Anyone that receives a child like this in my name receives me."* This is very similar to an old Eastern idiom that expresses the idea of one "who receives a child like I receive a child." It sounds almost like Jesus is saying that a child, in its innocent, natural way and unrestrained expression of the joy of the Lord, is God's way of directing us in our worship. It is very easy to turn our worship into a script and a method to keep things orderly and in control. We are told to stand, lift our hands, sing, close our eyes, etc., as an expression of true worship. Then in the midst of our nice, proper, holy stance, a child runs out and begins to express his or her joy by spinning around in a circle. Immediately the parent will lovingly put a restraining hand on the child and bring the child back into a proper stance that is less disruptive.

As I observed this child in this worship service, I could not help but think that the Spirit in this father was instructing him to let the child alone so that God could pick her up like Jesus picked up that *tela'* in Mark and held that little *tela'* in His arms and love on her. I sensed that the father watching his daughter spinning around in a circle out of pure joy found his heart warmed. Maybe he realized it or not, but somehow his spirit knew that his daughter was in the arms of Jesus, and by letting Jesus receive his daughter, he was receiving Jesus Himself. In fact, although neither the father and I performed the proper functions of worship, standing, lifted hands, eyes closed, we were actually worshipping God through this little child. We were receiving from this child in God's name, and thus we were receiving the presence of God.

For you see, in Aramaic, the second time the word received is used, it is a different word from the first word used for received. It is the word *qaval,* which is identical to a Hebrew word for *received,* which is *laqak. Laqak* is used, as in II Kings 5:15, to indicate one being in the presence of a prophet, king, or God. I believe what Jesus was really saying in this passage is that anyone who will allow a child to come before the presence of God in the name of Jesus, even in childlike behavior, will themselves enter into the presence of God. As that father allowed his daughter to enter the presence of God, in her childlike way, this act brought him and this poor slob watching all this into His presence as well.

ADOPTION – 'IMUTS

John 15:15: *"Henceforth I call you not servants; for the servant knoweth not what his lord doeth: but I have called you friends; for all things that I have heard of my Father I have made known unto you."*

Ephesians 1:5: *"Having predestinated us unto the adoption of children by Jesus Christ to himself, according to the good pleasure of his will."*

It seems few people give much thought to our relationship with God. Yet, when you start meditating on it and examining these relationships in light of Semitic culture, things start to get a little muddied. At one point, we are God's servants, and He is our master. Then we are his friend, and then adopted children and then just children. In our culture, we have no problem with this. We are all these things wrapped up in one. In our culture, a servant is just an employee who gets paid for his services; a friend is someone who clicks "friend" on Facebook or someone to share a backyard BBQ with. An adopted child is legally a child to that adoptive parent despite the fact that the mother did not actually give birth to the child. Then we have a child who was birthed by the mother. The Greeks are more Western-minded like us, and they have no problem wrapping us up all in one package. A Semitic mindset, however, has a real problem with these distinctions. These were actual class distinctions.

In an earlier study, I talked about servants *'avada*, who were actually the property of their masters. We make the parallel today to an employee, but that is not a fair parallel. Today we cannot imagine owning a human being. So that comparison is hard for us in a Western mindset.

Where the real problem comes is in the role of an adopted child and birth child. In the eyes of God, an adopted child is the true child of the adopted parents as if they gave birth to that child. However, in the eyes of the child, parents, and others in the community, they see a difference. I have known many who talk of their birth mother but also speak about their adopted mother and father. But they explain it like this: "Oh, they are not my real parents, I mean they are, but my real mother and father are...." There has been and always will be a minor social stigma in being adopted. The adopted child will wonder why their birth parents did not want them, the parents wonder what kind of genes may be in that child, the child's friends will look upon the child a little differently (oh, that is not his real mother). It is not right, and hopefully, our culture is moving toward more tolerance.

However, culturally, I have a problem being an adopted child of God. I mean, I feel like God took pity on this poor little orphan and adopted me. Ain't God wonderful. Yet, I read that when I accepted Jesus as my Savior, I was not adopted; I was born again. That means I was actually born into the family of God like a child is born from a mother and father. I have all the spiritual genetic makeup of my Heavenly Father.

So why does Paul call us adopted children? In an earlier chapter, I established that in the Aramaic, a word for love is *racham* which means one who was born from the womb and loved by the birth mother who carried that child in her womb for nine months, and then that child is placed in her arms. There is a difference at that moment, not a lasting one but a difference nonetheless. The mother will love the adopted child as her own but will not have the experience of carrying that child in her womb for nine months. Thus, an adopted child cannot be *racham*. We are not adopted; we are true birthed children of God who were racham, carried in the womb, and given birth, i.e., born again. As a mother suffers pain in childbirth, Jesus suffered the pain of the cross in giving us birth into His family.

In that case, we have a real contradiction in Scripture if we are adopted rather than born into the family of God. What is the real concept of being born again in this case?

Well, back to the Aramaic. What people call contradictions in the New Testament can most likely be resolved in the Aramaic, the language that Jesus spoke, the language that was Paul's native language. In the Aramaic version of the Bible, the Peshitta, the word adopt, is not found in this text or any other text in the New Testament that speaks of adoption.

Ephesians 1:5 Reads in Greek and English: *"Having predestinated us unto the adoption of children by Jesus Christ to himself...."* In Aramaic, it reads: *"Having predestinated us to be children of Jesus Christ to himself...."*

Why does the Greek text insert the word adoption? For one thing, I haven't yet found the Aramaic word for adopt. Perhaps it does not exist. Perhaps no distinction was made between an adopted child and one born into the family. I have my theories again, my own speculations. I believe the original text did not have the word adoption, and it was added later, perhaps when translated from the Aramaic into Greek. But many would disagree, so I only give it to you for your consideration. If you like the idea of being adopted by God, go with it. If you would rather be a child born into the family of God, you have a possible biblical basis for that. Choose what you want either way when we get to heaven; it won't matter one bit which theory you choose.

60

TAKE NO THOUGHT – YITSEPH

Matthew 6:31-32: *"Therefore take no thought, saying, What shall we eat? or, What shall we drink? or, Wherewithal shall we be clothed? (32) (For after all these things do the Gentiles seek:) for your heavenly Father knoweth that ye have need of all these things."*

This sounds like pretty bad advice that Jesus is giving His disciples. Take no thought about what you will eat? I mean, you really have to give it some thought. That is especially true in our days when we are watching our diets. Every time we go shopping we give some thought to what we will eat. It was also true in ancient times; eating and drinking were always on someone's mind. Starvation and dying of thirst took many lives in those days. Water was and is still a very precious commodity in the Near East. One was always thirsty. The acquisition of food was foremost on one's mind, and one had to carefully plan and ration foods when there were times of sacristy, which was very common. To say you should give no thought to what you will eat or drink was foolish. You had to plan well ahead of time to make sure you would be able to obtain food items and fresh water. To even clothe yourself was a constant worry. Only the rich had more than one set of clothes. Bandits would descend and rob a person just for the clothes on their backs and their one pair of sandals. You lived in constant fear of being robbed and left naked with no clothes. To give it no thought was bad advice.

The word in Greek for *take no thought* has almost an identical meaning as the Aramaic word. In Greek, the word is *merimnesete* from the root word *merimnaho*. The Aramaic word is *yitseph,* and both mean to be worried or to fret over something to the point where you are distracted from the business at hand. But, I have found in extra-biblical literature that the Aramaic word *yitseph* is also a word used for *fear* as in *fear* for one's own safety and well-being. This is distinct from the word *yara'* which is used for fear of the Lord which is a *fear* for the well-being of another. Fear for oneself is *pachad*. In other words, one fears the Lord as in fearing that they may wound His heart, break His heart or bring Him sadness.

Jesus is not saying that we should not plan for our next meal or what clothes we should wear; what He is saying is don't let your concern for these things distract you from your service to God. For most of us in the Western world, eating, drinking water, and having clothes is not a daily concern. Food is so plentiful that Ancient Near Eastern people would be aghast at the way we waste water and amazed that a person would get robbed and all the thief took was a small pouch with some paper in it. For the most part, we do not worry where our next meal will come from, nor do we give any thought as to our need for water and our only fear regarding clothes is that we wear an appropriate outfit for the appropriate occasion.

That phrase: *"For after all these things do the Gentiles seek,"* is very revealing as to the context in which Jesus is speaking. The word Gentiles is not used in the Greek or Aramaic. In Greek, it is the word *ethnos* where we get our English word *ethnic*. It is a word used for a different nationality or race of people. However, I believe that is not what Jesus was referring to. He spoke this in Aramaic, and the Aramaic words used were not referencing people of a different race, nationality, or religion. The words are *ammeh dalma*, which means worldly or fleshly people. Of course, everyone living in this world is made of flesh, so what is the distinction? What we have here in the words *ammeh dalma* is an Aramaic euphemism for people whose thoughts and concerns are only of this world and not of the spiritual world. It is an expression used for one who is so focused on an issue that he has little concern for the other issues around him.

What Jesus is saying is that we live in this world, we have to eat and drink water, we need to wear clothes, but if we seek the kingdom of God first, all these things will be outside our focus, and God has taken care so when we go into the "zone" of focusing on God and our mission from Him, when we come out of our zone, we will see His earthly provision.

Jewish men will wear a skull cap all day long. They do this to remind themselves that they are always in the presence of God and that all they do, they do as unto God. That skull cap is a reminder that they are not *ammeh dalma*, a worldly person or one whose thoughts and focus are on the things of the flesh but are on eternal things.

HOSANNA – HOSHI'AH

Matthew 21:9: *"And the multitudes that went before, and that followed, cried, saying, Hosanna to the Son of David: Blessed [is] he that cometh in the name of the Lord; Hosanna in the highest."*

Psalm 118:25: *"Save now, I beseech thee, O LORD: O LORD, I beseech thee, send now prosperity."*

On Palm Sunday, we celebrate the triumphal entry of Jesus in Jerusalem. Many people gathered Palm branches to wave and lay before Jesus as he rode into Jerusalem on a donkey. The Palm branches were used during the celebration of the liberation of the Jews by the Maccabees. We find this in I Maccabees 13:51. This victory is celebrated in the Jewish holiday of Hanukkah. Hence we call this Palm Sunday as that was one distinction of that day where everyone at church gets a palm branch. Actually, it would be more accurate to call it Donkey Sunday, and everyone gets a little plastic donkey, as the donkey was what was really predicted from Scripture in *Zechariah 9:9*: *"Rejoice greatly, O daughter of Zion; shout, O daughter of Jerusalem: behold, thy King cometh unto thee: he [is] just, and having salvation; lowly, and riding upon an ass, and upon a colt the foal of an ass."* However, I doubt it would carry the same flair as Palm Sunday, and besides, adolescents would want to use the "A" word rather than donkey.

There was something else predicted in Zechariah 9:9, the King arriving with salvation. The fame of Jesus had spread throughout Judea, and people began to talk. A rumor started that this was the Messiah and he was heading for Jerusalem. Like all prophetic people, they began to spread the rumor that this was the fulfillment of Zechariah 9:9 and He would arrive on a donkey to declare salvation (this might have been started by the chief priest). Most people equated salvation with deliverance from the Roman Empire. They would not have been the first prophetic people to mix up the prophetic signs.

However, this is the reason the people brought out the palm branches, expecting another deliverance like with the Maccabees. And no, they did not turn against Jesus a week later. They were just quickly silenced like a political supporter of an unpopular candidate. They had their cancel culture in those days as well. The court area of those who cried "Crucify Him!" was filled with paid agitators, egged on by the chief priest and his supporters. The court where Pilate stood was pretty small, and the only ones who were allowed to enter were those approved by the Chief Priest. Mel Gibson's movie *The Passion of the Christ* had it right, showing guards turning the true supporters of Jesus away. It was what we call today a Kangaroo court. The Jews hated capital punishment, and the Talmud is filled with so many legal obstructions to the laws of capital punishment that it became virtually impossible to execute someone under Jewish law. Hence the crime of treason had to be leveled against Jesus to get Him executed by the Romans, which, oddly enough, the triumphal entry proved to be perfect evidence of treason. I won't put it past the chief priest to have staged the whole thing to build a case of treason against Jesus and ironically use the people's adoration of Him to do it.

Most incriminating evidence came not only from the palm branches reflecting liberation but also from the shout of Hosanna. You probably learned from your preacher or priest that Hosanna is a proclamation of praise. That is confusing Hosanna with Hallelujah, although colloquially, it can mean praise. But to the first-century Jews is meant something else. Bible scholars believe the word was taken from Psalm 118:25, and people were actually quoting this Psalm. The first word is *hoshi'ah* which means save now. This comes from the root word *yasha'*, where you get the name *Yeshua*, Joshua, or Jesus. It means salvation. However, to the mind of the first century Jew, salvation did not indicate a spiritual matter but a political matter. Throughout the Old Testament, it talks of being saved and salvation, and we Christians simply related it to getting saved or born again when in the mind of the writer, it meant deliverance from a foreign enemy.

This word *yasha'* in Aramaic is in a causative form and means to be delivered, rescued, or saved. Hence it means "do something to bring about our deliverance." The word is in an imperfect form and could read as "you will deliver us" or as most translators believe as I do that the Hei at the end is a paragogic Hei which is an intensifier, thus: "Save us now." The word is really a compound word. *yehsaha* and *anna*. The internet calls *anna* as a plea or pleas. This is not entirely correct. It comes from the root word *ani* or *anah*, which means to answer or respond. It can be taken as a plea expressing a strong desire for an answer as "please respond."

Put together, Hosanna would translate out as "Please answer our prayer for deliverance." Of course: "Save now" also works.

62
GEHENNA

Matthew 5:29: *"And if thy right eye offend thee, pluck it out, and cast [it] from thee: for it is profitable for thee that one of thy members should perish, and not [that] thy whole body should be cast into hell."*

I remember hearing this verse read as a child and being very disturbed over it. Not the idea of plucking out your eye. Even at an early age, I had sense enough to know it was just a figure of speech and not to be taken literally. What really bothered me was the idea that if you didn't deal with this eye problem, you would be cast into hell. I mean, that sounds like we have to do more than just trust in the saving grace of Jesus to avoid hell; we actually have to take matters into our own hands and deal with our sins. That was scary, but even more disturbing is that it sounds like a real contradiction. On the one hand, I am told that it is by grace we are saved, through faith, that not of ourselves it is a gift of God, Ephesians 2:8-9. On the other hand, Jesus is commanding us to deal with the lust of the eye lest we end up in hell.

I think I was just twelve years old when I asked my pastor about this. I even set up an appointment to meet with him in his office to discuss this disturbing contradiction in the Bible. I mean, I had to know, am I saved by grace alone and not by any works I do, or am I required to keep my eye and hand from offending lest I go to hell. My pastor, a Bible college and seminary graduate, patted me on the head and said, "Oh, you are saved by grace alright, trust me that is what the church teaches, so don't worry about Matthew 5:29 there are many difficult passages in the Bible, and you are too young to understand, and you need a lot of education to understand such things. Great men of God have studied the Bible, and clearly, the Bible teaches you are saved just by the grace of God."

Well, sorry, my man, I was not about to trust in him or the church. My only trust would be in Jesus Christ, and if I could understand a contradiction at the age of twelve, then I should be able to understand an explanation. I suspected that even with his Bible College and seminary education, he didn't understand it either. So, I set out on a lifelong journey to get that education. I went to what I believed to be the best evangelical Bible College and Seminary I could find, and they did not give me an answer.

I finally went to a Jewish rabbi who was born and raised in the Middle East, and he had an answer. He simply asked me, "When you say, 'doggone it,' do you really mean a dog has gone? Gone where? You, Western people, don't make a lick of sense. What do you mean 'lick of sense?' How do you lick a sense?" Then he leaned forward and said, "Just as you have your idioms in English, we have ours in the Eastern world. In Semitic culture, the *eye* is the symbol of envy and desire. People in the Eastern world will often say, 'cut your eye from my ten camels.' To use that phrase in the Western world makes no sense, like *doggone it* or *lick of sense* does to the Eastern culture. What they are saying is don't envy my ten camels over your one camel.

Ok, I always knew to *pluck your eye out* was just an idiomatic expression, and the good rabbi clarified that this expression referred to envy. But, even Christian commentators have waxed lyrical on this in many ways. They talk of the mention of the right eye as a reference to that which is most dear to you. They speak of the concept of the *evil eye,* or they say it is the eye that excites thoughts of lust and envy, etc. All good explanations, and clearly, you do not literally pluck out your eye.

Ok, we all understand this. What my concern was that if we do not control the eye, we would end up in hell. What the rabbi said next may be misleading, so let me just say right here that I am still an evangelical, and I believe the Bible teaches that there is an afterlife and that we will spend it either in a place called heaven or a place called hell. Nor am I saying hell is not a place of eternal fires. I believe the Bible does teach this. However, I do not believe every time the word hell is used in the Bible that it is a reference to the afterlife. We must carefully look at the context to determine if the word hell is a reference to the afterlife and being used in a real literal sense or if it is just a reference to our physical life and is used in a metaphoric sense.

Aramaic Word Study

The word *hell* that is used in the Greek in Matthew 5:29 is the word *gehennan*, which is just a transliteration of the Hebrew word *gehinnom*. We call this Gehenna, which we all know is a reference to the garbage dump outside Jerusalem, which is constantly burning. Jesus was speaking in Aramaic, and the word he used was *gehana'*, which has no Hebrew root equivalent and in the Aramaic is a reference to metaphoric *Valley of sorrow and lamentations* or the *Valley of Baka' (weeping)* from Psalms 84:6. In Near Eastern culture, people do not take the word *hell* as literally as we do in the West. Most often, when the word falls on Semitic ears, they are hearing a metaphor as a reference to *mental suffering, anguish, regret, or a burning desire and passion.*

Let's back up to that word offend as in your eye offending you. The word used in Aramaic for *offend* is *keshal*, used in a hiphal form and means to *cause to stumble*. Thus, if your right eye is in the habit of lusting or envying, stop or break that habit before you suffer mental anguish and regret. I believe the context that Jesus is making a reference to is one of our life here on earth and not the afterlife; hence we need to view hell, in this verse, in a metaphoric sense as *mental anguish or a burning desire.*

Just an afterthought here. Let's suppose eternal hell is a place of mental anguish and burning lustful desires. Suppose someone's life's passion was alcohol, drugs, sex, material things? He spent no time building on eternal things such as a love for God, a desire for the presence of God. When we die, we get what we craved here on earth. If our craving was for alcohol, drugs, or sex, we need a physical body to satisfy that craving. But you will have no physical body like that on earth after death; thus, you will spend eternity tormented over a desire that can never be quenched in a spiritual state or spiritual body. That can be a hell more tormenting than fire. You will spend eternity just crying out for a drop of water on your tongue, but alas, you have no tongue. However, if your desires and passions were on a spiritual level, a desire to love God with all your heart, soul, and strength, a desire for the overwhelming presence of God. In eternity that desire will be even greater; only you will finally have that desire fulfilled and satisfied because you no longer have a physical body getting in the way.

As my grandpa used to say, it is like two dogs inside of you fighting, one evil or, in this case, one that is physical and the other one good, or in this case, the one that is spiritual. Which one wins out after we no longer have a physical earthly body? It will be the one we have fed the most.

WASHING HANDS – SHUG 'AIDA

Matthew 15:2: *"Why do thy disciples transgress the tradition of the elders? for they wash not their hands when they eat bread."*

In Matthew 15, the Pharisees accused Jesus of violating the Tradition of the Fathers by not instructing His disciples to wash their hands before eating bread. This had nothing to do with good hygiene. The Tradition of the Fathers, as found in the present-day Talmud, took the Scriptures like Deuteronomy 18:10-12 declaring that consulting familiar spirits, necromancy, enchanting, and witchcraft were an abomination to God and twisted them around to make it actually permissible as found in Sanhedrin 65a-b.

They actually cited the very Scriptural passage and reversed it, presenting the idea that it was ok to call up demons or spirits to come to your aid with sorcery as this is not idolatry since the demons were not being worshipped. Yeah, I know, bad Talmud, and I agree. Not only that, but Jesus also agreed this was not good and, in fact, a violation of the law of Moses. This is what Jesus was blasting the Pharisees about in Matthew 15. The Tradition of the Fathers/Talmud teaches that at night the demons will overcome a person when sleeping, and when he awakes, the demonic spirit moves into one's hands and the tips of his fingers (really, I'm not making this up). It was taught that the demons lived in water and loved water (remember the pigs that Jesus sent the demons into, and they ran off a cliff into the water?).

So, the sages taught that you needed to pour water over your hands three times to wash the demons away, especially before eating; you wanted to wash any remnants of the demons away before you passed the demon to your bread and then ingest the demons. This may sound crazy, but remember, they had no concept of microbes in those days, so when a person got sick after eating, they just assumed a demon got into him. The Pharisees explained every ill as something demonic, which today we know as simply a virus or a microbe. Thus their Tradition of the Fathers observed that a person who washed his hands before eating did not come down with an illness, so they assumed remnants of the demons were in your hands, and you needed to sprinkle water over your hands, and since the demons prefer water over a physical body you will, in fact, wash out the demons. Actually, if we were to insert the word demon for microbes and viruses, you could understand how a primitive culture would come to associate the effects of microbes to demons. I honestly do not know of any Jew who buys into this, but it was really popular among the Pharisees in Jesus' day.

So, in Matthew 15, Jesus is blasting the Pharisees for twisting the commandments of God around to the point where they were breaking the commandments and then accusing Jesus of breaking the Tradition of the Fathers, which was violating the commandments. Jesus really had His hands full.

We sort of chuckle over the ignorance of the first-century man while we play with a cheap aluminum cross we keep in our pockets because we believe it will somehow protect us. We pay our tithe believing such outward acts will make us prosperous; we attend church every Sunday because we just want to be sure we have enough points to make it into heaven.

If you think about it, you will find that we can be just as foolish as the people of the first century who thought washing your hands would wash away demons.

64

WOMAN – 'ANATH

John 2:4: *"Jesus said unto her, Woman what have I to do with thee, my hour has not yet come."*

Woman: Aramaic (Syriac) 'anath – a married woman, a woman who is not a virgin. Greek: gunai – a married woman

In the King James Version rendering of this verse, it sounds like Jesus was being very harsh, rude, and disrespectful to His mother. Indeed, we tend to lose a lot in translation. Even if the Book of John were not written in Aramaic, John would have taken his notes in Aramaic, and the conversation would have been in Aramaic. Hence the Syriac version of the Bible would carry a more correct or better understanding of the word woman that is used here. The word rendered as woman is *'anath* in Aramaic, and the Greek rendering, which is *gunai* seems to be in agreement. He was addressing his mother as a married woman. *'Anath* is a married woman or a woman who is not a virgin, and the Greek is simply a married woman.

One would have to ask, would not simply saying the Aramaic word for mother, which is *'amah* which would accomplish the same thing and been more respectful? I do have a pet theory. The Aramaic word, *'amah*, sounds an awful lot like the Hebrew word 'almah, which means an unmarried woman, either she has never been married or was widowed. In some cases, it might refer to a woman who was divorced or abandoned. This is the same word used in Isaiah 7:14, which was a double prophecy and spoke of an *'almah* or virgin who will conceive and bear a son. There would be a fulfillment in Ahaz's time as a sign that his enemies would be destroyed by God as well as a future event of a coming Messiah who would be born of a virgin. The word *alamah* was an excellent choice of words for this prophecy as it could mean both a virgin and non-virgin. The term would be used for a non-virgin but an unmarried woman who bore a son during Ahaz's time and a virgin, Mary, who bore the Messiah.

Perhaps in this story in Matthew where Jesus calls his mother "woman," Jesus was making a little play on words hinting a little secret shared only between He and His mother at that time, that is, that He was the Son of God in fulfillment of Isaiah 7:14 and maybe He would do a little miracle to sort of set the stage for His entry into His Messianic mission. Sort of a coming-out party.

On the other hand, calling His mother *'anath* in Aramaic was really a sign of respect in that culture. Joseph would have most likely died at this point but not before Mary had other children and would thus no longer be a virgin. In a sense, Jesus was doing her an honor calling her an 'amah as this would be declaring that she was a single mother by the death of her husband, who raised her children under the hardship of widowhood. I have heard successful men and women speak with pride for their mothers when they say: "My mother was a single mother and raised me." I think the NIV, which did a little paraphrasing, expressed it best – "Dear woman."

The expression "my hour has not yet come" is really an Aramaic idiom. The BYOB concept was a common practice at oriental weddings, with everyone male bringing his own brew and trying to show off that he had the best wine. Maybe the other women were starting to give Mary a hard time that her son did not bring any wine to the wedding as was the custom. Mary may have been keeping a little secret that her son was going to offer the best wine ever. Jesus' response to His mother in the Aramaic was literally: "what to you and to me, not yet woman." Again, my pet interpretation of that phrase, based upon what I view as the context, would be almost conspiratorial: "What we talked about dear woman, but not yet – patience." With a little knowing and maybe the smugness of a proud mother, she went to the attendants and instructed them to do whatever Jesus said. She knew what Jesus proposed to do would be a bit strange, and she had to prepare the servants. Jesus was going to use the water in the vessels that the guest used to wash their hands and feet in before the meal. When he ordered the servants to fill the vessels, he was saying to add water to replace the water splashed out during the bathing. Keep in mind, people did not wash their hands and feet for hygienic purposes in those days; they did it for ritualistic purposes as required by Jewish law to symbolize purification or cleansing. Jesus was going to demonstrate His role as the Messiah by taking the filth and dirt and purifying it.

Still, people washing their hands and feet after traveling through dusty roads can make the water pretty rank. That is probably why Jesus waited until the last hour to introduce his BYOB. In Oriental culture, it was a sign of good hospitality to get you totally bombed at a wedding, and Jesus was probably waiting until the guests were too drunk to care if they were drinking bath water or not.

I suspect John recorded this story to declare to the world and future generations that Jesus came to this world to take all its grimy, stinking filth and purify it into pure good wine.

By the way, as a side note, the Talmud clearly defines the number of days that wine was to be fermented for various occasions. For a wedding, the fermentation was only to be three or four days, and according to those I have spoken with who apparently know, that is not enough time to ferment wine into cough syrup. Good wine was a wine that followed the guidelines of proper fermentation procedures for ceremonial wine.

65

TRUTH

John 8:32: *"And you shall know the truth, and the truth shall set you free."*

I used to love to have arguments –uh, discussions with my Jehovah Witness friends. Invariably we would approach an impasse such as John 1:1, which they render as "The Word was a god." They would argue that in the Greek, there is no definite article in front of the word God, so, therefore, it must be rendered as "a god." I would throw out that in the Greek, when you have two nominatives (in this case, logos and Theos) that have the same ending in the same sentence, the grammatical way of determining the direct object is to add the definite article (ho) to the subject and leave it off the direct object. Even though logos comes at the end of the sentence, we do not assume logos is the subject, like in English, as the order of words does not determine the subject or predicate. Therefore, John was only using good grammar by making it clear that the subject was logos and not Theos, so we would properly render the verse as "The Word was God" and not "God was the Word."

Well, at that point, they would come back with their ace in the hole and say: "But we teach the truth." Then I would throw out my trump card by pulling a Pilate and asking: "What is truth." Actually, I didn't know any more than they did what I was talking about when I used the word truth, but if "you can't convince 'em, confuse 'em," as my old Theology professor would say. But then again, maybe they understood that word *truth* better than I did. When they said they had the truth, they were saying that they only were expressing what they believed God revealed to them personally. I feel I need to take a better look at this word truth.

So once more, with lexicon in hand, I return to my quest to understand those words we use so often but do not understand, such as *truth*. This time I will examine it in the Aramaic, and John 8:32 is a good place to start. According to this verse, it is truth that will make you free, and I like freedom.

Actually, the expression: "The truth shall make you free" is an old Jewish saying that predates Jesus and was in common use during His time. Oral tradition, later recorded in the Talmud, that "No man was free but he that exercises himself in the meditation of the law." Jesus was most likely addressing this study of the law and coming to a proper understanding of the law.

The word for *free* in Greek is *eleutherosei,* which means to liberate or release from captivity. In the Aramaic, the word is *harar*, which means *to think*. In Hebrew, the word *harar* means much the same, but as a noun, it means a mountain. In a feminine form, it means a pregnant woman. Not that the woman is large like a mountain, but that a mountain was representative of a place you go to meditate, think, and draw closer to God. Before they knew about raging hormones, a pregnant woman was thought to be closer to the mind of God because she had been granted a miracle (giving of life) by God. Hence this word that is used for *free* in the Aramaic has the idea of independent thinking. In this context, it is thinking that is independent of the teachings of the fathers who gave their personal interpretation as to what the law meant and how to apply it. When you know the truth, you will understand the law of God for yourself and not have to rigidly follow man's interpretation, regardless of how learned or smart that person may be. Man's interpretation can be a guide, but ultimately you or the revelation inside you makes the decision.

So what is truth? There is an interesting play on words here. The word *truth* in Greek is *aletheia,* which is used to describe, you guessed it, truth. It is also used for reality, sincerity, and divine revelation. In the Aramaic, however, we see a subtle play on words. The Aramaic word used here is identical to the Hebrew word *sharar.* Freedom is spelled "Hei, Resh, Resh" truth is spelled "Shin, Resh, Resh. The words are spelled the same, except one starts with a Hei and the other starts with a Shin. The word sharar means to be firm by twisting and tightening. It also means to rule or command. An age-old teaching about leadership is to make a decision, stand firmly and tight by that decision, and accept responsibility for that decision.

I believe what Jesus is saying here is that He is truth, He is the commander of what is and what is not, He will not change nor alter his position, and he accepts full responsibility for the consequences of his instructions or commands. Yet, to follow His instructions, you will receive orders from no one else, you will have the freedom to think on your own. In other words, you can make the decision as to how to interpret the law. You will decide if walking a mile on the Sabbath is breaking the Sabbath or not or if eating pork to survive when no other food is available is breaking the dietary laws or saying "That dress looks fantastic on you" when you hate it is a lie or not. Let the "Truth," the Jesus who lives inside you, decide. As Jimmy Cricket would say: "Let your conscience be your guide." In this case, your conscience is the Jesus who lives inside of you.

Oh, by the way, that play on words. The difference between the word *truth (sharar)* and *freedom (harar)* is that one has a Shin, which represents the power and passionate love of God, and the other has a Hei, which represents the presence of God. When you accept Jesus as the *sharar (truth)* in your life or your authority and not man's, then you will have the freedom to receive His passionate love, power, and presence. With that, you can move a *harar* (mountain).

GOOD (SHEPHERD)

John 10:11: *"I am the good shepherd; the good shepherd gives his life for his sheep."*

Greek: kalos - beautiful, fine, excellent, blameless, high moral character.

Aramaic: tawa' – A relationship with someone or something that is harmonious and in sync.

Jesus calls himself a good shepherd. There are a few words in Greek that are rendered as good and about four words in Aramaic rendered as good. The Aramaic words hana (pleasurable, beautiful, find) and taqan (honest, blameless, high moral character) would best match the Greek word kalos that is used in John 10:11. However, the Aramaic New Testament uses the word tawa' (perfect harmony) instead. Jesus spoke these words in Aramaic, and John heard them in Aramaic and perhaps translated them into Greek if he did not write them down in Aramaic first.

So why was the word kalos chosen? I reviewed all the words I could find in the Greek that could be rendered as good, and none really expressed the basic idea of *tawa'*, which is similar to the Hebrew word *tov*. Hence the Greek writer could only choose the best possible Greek word for *tawa,'* and even that falls short.

The Aramaic word *tawa'* is rooted in a relationship. In review of all the Greek words, I could not find any that would actively speak of a relationship. All, more or less, address one's character, courage or appearance. Yet, the whole idea of Jesus illustrating Himself as a shepherd carries the idea of a relationship and really speaks little of his appearance, moral character, or courage. Perhaps the word "good" is not our best rendering, although I, for one, would never be a part in tearing down this iconic expression. I like calling Him the Good Shepherd, but we really need to define "good."

There were two types of shepherds in Jesus' day. There were the hired shepherds and the self-employed shepherds who owned their own sheep. In the ancient Eastern culture, a shepherd was a highly respected occupation. Women desired to see their sons become shepherds. If a man had no sons, he would be forced to hire a stranger to watch his sheep. This was not the best option as shepherding was a very hazardous job. A shepherd had to protect a bunch of senseless animals from attack by wolves, bandits, hostile weather, and any number of threats. The first sign of a bunch of knife welding thieves and a hired shepherd will say: "Risk my life for room and board? I'm out of here." However, if a man's personal livelihood is threatened, that is a threat to his wife, children, and his future, he would take the risk. I remember a movie where the director of a hospital was locked out of his hospital by armed radicals. The director pointed to a couple security guards and said: "Ok, come on, we're going to take these guys." The security guard said: "At $7.50 an hour, are you crazy?"

There were plenty of courageous, honorable hired shepherds, but they did not have a relationship with their sheep; their relationship was with their paycheck. Get fired from one shepherd job; they just moved to another community; background checks were difficult in those days.

Jesus is not only our Good Shepherd, or the Shepherd who is not into it for the paycheck and will abandon his sheep the first time one wanders off a dangerous cliff or faces hungry wolves, but He has also set Himself up as a role model for Christian leaders. How many pastors would walk into a crack house and bodily pick up one of the young people from his church and drag him home? How many pastors would get up in the middle of the night during a snowstorm and drive to the bedside of a church member who needs his hand held and prayer? How many pastors would take a pay cut during a recession so members of His congregation would not be burdened with dipping into their unemployment checks?

In other words, how many pastors are truly *tawa'* shepherds (good shepherds) and not hired shepherds who will abandon their sheep at the first sign of trouble or the offer of a bigger church and more pay?

REBUKE – KA'A

Luke 9:55: *"But he turned and rebuked them and said, ye know not what manner of spirit ye are of."*

I have sat through a number of Bible studies and Sunday School classes where a verse similar to this is read, and someone raises their hand and says: "But my Bible does not say that." What follows is a brief pat answer from the leader about differences in translations. What gets dicier is a verse like Luke 9:55 where the KJV has the last phrase, *"ye know not what manner of spirit ye are of,"* but our modern translations, like the NIV, ESV, etc., do not. This usually sends the leader sputtering who really has no answer, at least one that can be given in a brief statement. I tend to keep my mouth shut during these questions as I am briefly transported back to my days in graduate school, where I studied textual criticism and how it led me to question my own faith and belief in the authority of the Scriptures. Yesterday I listened to a segment on the internet about a book that was guaranteed to convince the reader that the Bible is truly the Word of God. This book apparently went into something called: Bible Codes, and the "amazing" results of these Bible Codes professed to prove in no uncertain terms that the Bible is truly the inspired Word of God.

I am not about to waste $25.00 on a book of so-called Bible Codes to convince me that the Bible is the Word of God because I know no such evidence will convince me. I accept my Bible and the dozens of others in different translations sitting on my table right now as the true inspired Word of God by faith and faith alone.

So, what do I do with a passage like Luke 9:55 where my KJV includes that last phrase but other modern translations do not? I turn to my Aramaic Bible. You see, the problem lies in the use of the Greek manuscripts for translation. The KJV depended heavily upon the Textus Receptus, which is a group of fifth-century manuscripts used by Erasmus in 1512 to develop a standard Greek NT alongside the Latin Vulgate. Erasmus had access to only six manuscripts, all dated around the fifth century AD. Modern translators have access to far more manuscripts, some earlier, than the ones available to Erasmus and the translators of the KJV version. Modern translators use the Nestle-Aland Text or the Novum Testamentum Graece, which is the standard Greek text used by all Evangelical Bible Colleges and Seminaries. This Greek New Testament is based upon a much broader range of manuscripts. This is known as the critical text or eclectic text, which refers to a committee that decided what manuscripts were closest to the original Greek manuscripts since the originals are believed to no longer exist. They look at the date of the manuscripts (earlier, the better), the geographical location where the manuscripts originated, and the accidental or intentional corruption of the manuscripts. Putting this all together, the committee voted and agreed as to what was the closest to the original. In this case, the last phrase of Luke 9:55 did not make the final cut, so it was, therefore, declared not a part of the inspired Word of God. In graduate school, I was involved with the translation of the New International Version (NIV). I have since heard it referred to as the New Inspired Version. I do laugh in private as I wonder if this criticism is not accurate.

The bottom line is which version has it right. Did Jesus actually say to James and John: "You do not know what manner of spirit you are of?" We really do not know.

As this battle for the Greek Bible went on in the Western world and the Western church, the Eastern church (Greek Orthodox today) did not suffer such turmoil. One big reason for this is that, unlike the Western church, the Jewish people were accepted. In the Western Church, Constantine (306-337) eased the Jews out of the church as he developed the Roman Catholic church or Western Church. Constantine sought to unify Europe and to create one religion, and a key to this was to incorporate many pagan ideas into the church to create this unity. The Jews could not accept this and left, leaving Constantine to develop the church without any Jewish influence and moving Scripture out of its Semitic roots into Latin and Greek. One of the great mysteries of the Greek New Testaments is the disappearance of the original manuscripts, and only those that date to the time of Constantine can be found. Not to accuse Constantine of tampering with the Bible but kicking the Jews out of the church and losing the original manuscripts does create a smoking gun in my mind.

The Eastern church, however, retained its Semitic origins and welcomed Jewish Christians, and it is the teaching of the Eastern Church that the New Testament was written in Aramaic, the language of Jesus, a Semitic language common to all Jews and then was later translated into Greek a non-Semitic language. This is one of the reasons for this book and why I spend time studying the Peshitta alongside the Greek New Testament, and I let the Holy Spirit guide me to the understanding He is leading me into. At this stage, I do not find anything contradictory between the Aramaic and the Greek. I just find a little broader understanding.

The Aramaic Bible does retain this phrase by Jesus: "you know not what manner of spirit you are of" however, it is clearly an idiomatic expression used even today in the Middle East to express the idea: "You don't realize how angry you are." James and John, like many of us today, will deny our anger and feel justified in our actions. We say things like: "I am not angry; I am just pointing out a fact." In truth, Jesus pointed out to these two disciples, the sons of thunder, you are angry, you are speaking out of anger. The word "rebuke" in Greek is *epetimesen*, which means to censure or admonish. In the Aramaic, the word is *ka,a*, which is very similar to the Hebrew word *ka'ah*, which means to feel despondent or to grieve in your heart. The Aramaic word also means to rebuke, but it is a verbal expression of despondency.

In other words, Jesus did not scold James and John, as the Greek text would suggest, but only expressed his inner grief over their reaction. Here he has laid bared his heart to his disciples, his love for mankind, and James and John are ready to potty-train the Samaritans with lightning bolts for their rejection. The tragedy is that James and John thought they were being very pious and righteous following the example of Elijah, when all the time they were just angry and vengeful.

Maybe there is a play on words here; maybe there is an evil spirit that blinds us to our bitterness and anger and makes us believe we are being holy and pious when we call someone a toad and blast them out of the water. Yeah, we can say: "Oh, maybe I was a little angry here, but I was justified in it. I was doing it in love." Just as James and John were justified in their anger and even had Scripture to back them up. Yet it still caused James and John to *ka'a* - wound the heart of Jesus.

68
THE WAY

John 14:6: *"Jesus said, I am the way the truth and the life, no man comes to the father but by me."*

As a 12-year-old child, I recall attending the Billy Graham Crusade in Chicago. We attended every night of the crusade, and each night above the 3,000 voice choir, there stood a banner proclaiming the words: *"Jesus said, I am the way, the truth and the life, no man comes to the father but by me."* I made no conscious effort to memorize this verse; it just embedded itself in my memory as I observed this passage of Scripture every night for the two-week duration of the crusade.

It is no wonder that I have been fascinated with the words *way, truth, life, and Father* all my life. In Chapter 65, I did a study on the word *truth or sharar*. I indicated that the word *sharar* means to be firm by twisting and tightening. It also means to rule or command. I pointed out an ancient teaching about leadership that still exists today as being able to make a decision, stand firmly and tight by that decision and accept responsibility for that decision. What Jesus is saying when He says He is truth, is that He is the commander of what is and what is not, He will not change nor alter his position, and he accepts full responsibility for the consequences of his instructions or commands. I would like to add that this truth is spelled with a Shin, which tells us that truth contains the power and passionate love of God. The double Resh indicates that truth is the ultimate in leadership or headship. If a leader is not totally honest with those who follow his leadership, he will lose their respect, their loyalty, and their devotion, and when the time comes, they will question his commands and decisions.

Jesus also says He is the life. In the Aramaic, the word used for *life* is identical to the Hebrew word *chi,* which means physical life, quality of life, and spiritual life. The word in Aramaic ends with an Aleph, which indicates a definite article. Hence He is *the life.* He is the controlling factor in not only our physical life, when it begins and when it ends, but the quality of life as well. Not only that, He is the controlling factor in our spiritual life and the ultimate destination or destiny of our spiritual life. To say He is *chi'a* (the life) is a claim no one, not even the angels in heaven can make.

Finally, He says that He is the *way.* The word in Greek is *hodos* which means way, road, or path. Yet, Jesus spoke the words in the Old Galilean dialect of Aramaic, and the word used has a little twist in it that the Greek does not or cannot give. The word in Aramaic is *urcha. Hodos* is the closest Greek word you can get to it, yet no word in Greek can convey the one other rendering or use of the Aramaic word *urcha,* which would more easily fit the context of this verse. That is the word *religion.* Religion is, after all, nothing more than the way to the Father, which is the context of this verse. Hence Jesus is saying that He is *the religion.* That little Aleph at the end of that word destroys any notion that Islam, Judaism, Hinduism, Buddhism, and yes, even Christianity is the true religion. There is no religion in the world that is the true (*sharar*) religion. Jesus is plainly saying in Aramaic that He is the only one and true religion, the only way to the Father.

This brings us to the last word of interest in this verse, *Father.* The Greek uses the word *patera,* which means a father, elder, or senior. Again, the Aramaic word *avi* can mean father, elder, or senior, but that little Yod at the end of the word, that personal pronoun adds a little dimension to the word that you will not find in the Greek. *Avi* is used in the Old Galilean dialect by one who wishes to address another as "my beloved." All fathers, elders, or seniors may not be "beloved." I spoke with someone the other day whose father abused him and then abandoned him. He would scoff at the notion of calling his father an *avi* (beloved).

So, Jesus is saying that He is the true commander of our faith who will never change and who will bind Himself to use such that He will be the controlling factor in our physical as well as spiritual life and destiny and that He and He alone is the true religion, the only religion that will lead us to our beloved God, the God we wish to be with not for a better life, but simply because we love Him.

WHERE IS THY STING

I Corinthians 15:55-57: *"O death, where [is] thy sting? O grave, where [is] thy victory? The sting of death [is] sin; and the strength of sin [is] the law. But thanks [be] to God, which giveth us the victory through our Lord Jesus Christ."*

Deuteronomy 1:44: *"And the Amorites, which dwelt in that mountain, came out against you, and chased you, as bees do, and destroyed you in Seir, [even] unto Hormah."*

I remember when I first heard I Corinthians 15:55 quoted when I was a child and I sort of shuddered. Death has a sting to it? For some reason, that expression just never seemed right to me. Why was Paul referring to death with a sting? I am not sure what about it that bothered me, but it just never seemed right. Yet, every English translation I read uses the word sting. The word in Greek used for sting is *kentron*, which means to prick, a sharp point, and to sting.

Many commentators believe Paul was quoting *Hosea 13:14: "I will ransom them from the power of the grave; I will redeem them from death: O death, I will be thy plagues; O grave, I will be thy destruction: repentance shall be hid from mine eyes."* which seems to follow the same line of thought only it says "O death, I will be thy plagues, O grave, I will be thy destruction." Some say Paul misquoted this verse which would put the inspiration of Scripture in question. Others take you on a little linguistical tour and point out that sting and plagues really mean the same thing.

I went to the Aramaic version of the Bible, which was Paul's native language, and I found the word used for sting was *'aqats* which has the idea of bending and twisting. It is an agricultural term to forcibly removing the fruit of a vine or a tree by bending and twisting it. Rather than just let the fruit fall from the tree on its own, the harvester forces the fruit off the branch by pulling, twisting, and bending it. I suppose I could figure out some connection of this to verse, except that is how the word is used as a verb. In this passage, it is a noun, and as a noun, *'aqats* is used as the stinger on a bee and the idea of the bee twisting and bending his stinger to remove it, and it removes the stinger from itself and dies.

I thought of this when we were preparing for one of our Torah Portion studies for our Learning Channel. I remember reading in Deuteronomy 1:44: *"And the Amorites, which dwelt in that mountain, came out against you, and chased you, as bees do,"*

I was a camp director with my brother at a camp for inner-city children. We had a session for 6-8-year-olds. My brother and I were co-directors, and we would play bad cop, good cop to maintain discipline. Of course, you can guess who got to be the bad cop. I soon became known as Mr. Meany. At the beginning of the camping session, we all gathered around the flagpole, where I laid down the rules of the camp. One basic, fundamental rule was never to go into the woods without a counselor. Violators would get up to five checks on my clipboard. I never explained what the checks meant or the penalty for having too many checks as there was none. Just the idea alone of getting a check was deterrent enough. That is except for one camper. She was older than the rest (we could never prove it) and bigger, and was a bully. One day she convinced her entire cabin to go into the woods with her without a counselor. I was near the trail leading into the woods when I heard a dozen little girls screaming, and all of a sudden, I saw them running out of the woods, and right behind them was a swarm of bees. I sort of marveled at the fact that the bees followed them out of the woods. The bees were not satisfied to just chase them away from their hive; they insisted on chasing them all the way to the camp, and then they began to wage war against the whole camp. Just a little epilogue to this story. As the little girls were having their bee stings tended to by the camp nurse, they started to accuse Mr. Meany (me) of sending the bees to sting them because they disobeyed my order. Yep, that's me alright, I was so mean that I would sick bees on little girls to sting them for disobedience. Now I know how God must feel.

At first reading of Deuteronomy 1:44, if you are not a city slicker, you would guess that this is what it means when the Amorites chased Israel out of their land, they just kept following them until they reached their own camp. But according to Rashi, a medieval Jewish commentator, the ancients believed that when a bee stung you, it loses its stinger and dies, which is true for honey bees. His comment on this was that the Amorites were due to die once they lost their stinger like a bee. So too, with the believer, that if anyone tries to sting us or harm us, they will lose their stinger and eventually die.

But when I consider I Corinthians 15:55-57, I find this word *'aqats* fits very nicely as a noun. For we learn in this verse that sin is the stinger. In other words, we would read this as *"O Death, where is your stinger?"* The stinger is death's tool, but for the believer, death no longer has a stinger. As a believer we need never fear death for there is no sin in death, that sin is gone, removed by the blood of Jesus. End of life for the believer is merely a consummation of our marriage with God; the enemy no longer has his stinger, his weapon; he does not even have an invitation to our wedding with Jesus. The enemy is a bee without a stinger, no matter how hard he tries to afflict us with sin, he cannot penetrate the blood of Jesus, and he is just a docile little insect crawling around hopelessly trying to penetrate our souls with sin which he cannot do when it is covered by the blood of Jesus.

70

DEMON/MENTAL ILLNESS - DEWANA

Matthew 8:31: *"So the devils besought him, If thou cast us out, suffer us to go away into the herd of swine."*

"You American bum, we want picture of American bum, will give ten dollar for picture of American bum." **Japanese tourists overheard speaking to a homeless man in downtown Chicago**

Let me say at the outset that I do believe that demons can possess a human being. I worked for an evangelist and teacher who was known throughout the world for his deliverance ministry, and I do not question for a moment that Jesus cast demons out of people in his day as well as today. This man of God that I worked for, however, often warned not to look for demons under every bush. That was good advice as you may be addressing a physical problem or mental problem and not a demonic problem at all. You could end up doing more harm than good. You must use great spiritual discernment before you address a problem as demonic.

As I study the Gospels in the Aramaic, I am beginning to realize that same advice would apply to our study of the Scripture. There are cases where Jesus cast demons out of people, and there are cases where Jesus merely healed a person. The difference is not always clear in our Greek text, but in the Aramaic, it becomes very clear and also helps to resolve some mysteries.

This passage, I believe, is one example that should be studied in the Aramaic as it may answer a few questions. The word used for *devils* in Greek is *daimones*. Greek is a very precise language, and you have little choice but to render this word as *demon* or *devil*. In other words, the Greek word clearly applies to a supernatural spirit. However, the word used in Aramaic is *dewana*, which could mean a demon, or it could mean an insane or mentally ill person. People living in the Semitic regions in those days, as still today, consider every illness as demonic. Medical science has proven that this is not true, as we are now able to successfully treat many of these illnesses without casting a demon out of the person. I am cautious in saying that as there are cases that medical science cannot address and are only addressed through prayer, fasting, and commanding a demon to leave in the name of Jesus.

Still, that word in the Aramaic, *dewana,* does leave the door open to two possibilities. It could refer to demonic activity, or it could refer to just mental illness. Let's take this story, for instance. There are many questions that arise if we consider rendering *dewana* as demonic. First, in verse 29, we learn that these two *dewanas* were hiding out in a tomb, and when they saw Jesus, they cried out, "Jesus, thou Son of God, art thou come hither to torment us before our time?" First, it is not unusual that these men would have known or heard of Jesus as his fame was growing at this time. In verse 28, we learn that these men were Gararenes or Gentile Syrians. This area of Gararenes was known for raising pigs as their primary occupation. To call Jesus Son of God did not have the implications that those of a Hebrew heritage would have if they used that term. To the gentiles, any holy man was considered the son of a god.

The phrase, "torment us before our time" is a cultural phrase. If these men were mentally ill and not demon-possessed, then they were most likely referring to the *evening time* where these roaming mentally ill people were sometimes brought in and used for entertainment. They were made to sing, dance, and act in humiliating and foolish ways. The insane were free to roam about the towns and were constantly teased and tormented by certain individuals, not unlike many of the mentally ill and homeless are today in our cities. Because of their dress, and behavior they tend to become a source of amusing interest to certain people as I overhead from some Japanese tourist in downtown Chicago trying to get a picture of an "American bum."

If these men were simply mentally ill, they no doubt feared they were about to be used as a possible teaching illustration for this holy man and his disciples. However, these men then beseeched Jesus. If they knew His name, they knew His reputation as a healer, and they begged him: "If you cast us out...." The Greek word used here is *ekballo* which means to banish or cast out. Remember, these men would be speaking Aramaic and not Greek. The Aramaic word used here is *mapaq*, which comes from the root word *paqah*, which is identical to the Hebrew word and means to deliver or save. Thus, these men said: "If you would deliver us or heal us, allow us to go away into the herd of swine." The word in Aramaic used for *go away into* is simply *al*. This has the idea of attacking. It is often used today to express the idea of attacking. For instance, the word would be used in the sentence: "The wolves are *al* the sheep." We would render that as: "The wolves are entering into the sheep." But the Semitic people would understand that as the wolves attacking the sheep. Thus, these men, knowing how pigs were considered unclean to the Jews, were willing to prove their conversion by attacking the pigs and chasing them off the mountain.

I have always had two questions concerning this story, as seen in the Greek. First, why did the demons have to ask permission to enter into the pigs, the most unclean animals, but did not need permission to enter these men? Secondly, why go into pigs and then cause them to run off a mountain where their new home or possession was short-lived. Perhaps these men promised that if Jesus healed their mental torment, they would chase these pigs off the mountain and rid these unclean animals from His sight as their way of thanking Jesus for the healing.

Were these men demon-possessed or just mentally ill? I don't know. The answer may lie in how we render this passage from the Aramaic. I am not saying these men were not demon-possessed; I am merely pointing out another option and passing on a word of advice from my former employer, who was one of the leading teachers in the deliverance ministry – "Don't be looking for a demon under every bush - use deep spiritual discernment."

71

SIMULATED WORSHIP

II Timothy 3:1,5: *"This know also, that in the last days perilous times shall come. Having a form of godliness, but denying the power thereof: from such turn away."*

My great great grandfather, so I am told, came to America from Germany because of the wars and rumors of wars and found himself in the American Civil war. He thought it was the last days. My great grandfather struggled with poverty and plagues, convinced he was living in the last days. My grandfather fought in World War I and was convinced they were living in the last days. My father grew up during the Great Depression and then served in World War II and faced the threat of nuclear war and was convinced, without doubt, we were living in the last days. I grew up during the time of the cold war, the race riots, Lyndon Johnson's Great Society sending our country into billions of dollars of debt with such socialist programs as welfare, Medicaid, Medicare, and other social programs caring for the elderly and poor as Jesus taught. I was told this would bankrupt our country within ten years (It didn't, we only prospered). But, I was convinced we were living in the last days. Here we are again with political unrest, the threat of civil war (although not nearly on the scale of 1862), socialist programs that will bankrupt this country, pandemics, and people are crying out that we are living in the last days.

I would just like to address the elephant in the room here. Doesn't it seem like we are always living in the last days? There seems to have always been wars, rumors of wars, civil unrest, threats of national bankruptcy (Roosevelt the godfather of all free-spending on socialist programs), and political crisis? Just what makes up the last days? Perilous times? You don't think the 15th-century plagues, the crisis in the church during the 16th-century reformation, the many wars that practically wiped out Europe were perilous times?. Frankly, I will take our present perilous times over the perilous times of the 30-year war in Europe or our present COVID 19 pandemic over the bubonic plague of the 14th-century, which killed over half the population of Europe. Just what makes us think our perilous times are any more of an indication of last days than the perilous times throughout history which were obviously not the last days?

Of course, we could say the last days began with the resurrection of Jesus. Who is to say that in God's eyes, the last days could be 2,000 years. One day with the Lord is as a thousand years. Last days or last times in Greek is *eschatais hemerais* or extreme to the end days meaning literal sun up to sun down days. This is followed by the words *enstesontal kairoi*, which literally has the idea of presenting opportunities. *Kairoi* is traditionally rendered as times or seasons, but it could also mean opportunities followed by the word for hard or difficult, perhaps referring to difficult opportunities. These last days could really be days of great opportunity, if not difficult.

Let's examine this in the Aramaic, the language that was the writer's native tongue. Last days is *echadi zavana'*. The word *echadi* means one, but it also means to be unique or special. The word times is *zavana'*, which carries the definite article from *echadi* and means to sell off or sell out, to bargain. It has the idea of selling and buying, negotiating a deal. It is also a word for compromise. In other words, the last days could be rendered as a unique time of compromise or buying selling.

Verses 2-4 speak of people during these unique times who will be lovers of self, money, proud, arrogant, and so forth. People have always been this way. But verse 5 tells us what these people are; they are believers who have a form of godliness but deny the power of God. The word power in Greek is *dynamin*, which is miraculous power. In the Aramaic, it is *chayl*, which is similar to the Hebrew for dancing with joy and strength. In Aramaic, it means that as well as a word for supernatural strength, so it does not contradict the idea of miraculous power but expands on it by including the idea of joyfulness.

I believe that is what is important here. In the last days, believers are not just going to find it difficult to discover the joy of the Lord, but they will deny there is such a thing. What I see happening today is something called progressive Christianity, which teaches that you do not really feel the presence of the joy of the Lord; you are only feeling the natural excitement of spiritual music and working yourself up into a sense of joy as you do at an athletic event. But what you feel is not God. These preachers who call themselves evangelicals actually deny the *chayl*, the joy, celebration, and physical manifestations of God. Ok, there have always been those who teach this, they used to be called liberals and/or neo-orthodox, but the idea of last days in the Aramaic would be a unique time of sell-off, buy and sell. Perhaps it is not the last days but a time *of unique opportunities* when Christianity seeks to become acceptable to society. So as not to be accused of hate speech or be offensive, they seek what is not offensive to non-believers. They don't talk of the blood of Jesus, blood is offensive, or hold up a cross that is offensive to those who are not Christians. Oh, and Heaven forbid that you should tell someone they are a sinner; why, that is hate speech. By the way, any sane person knows not to tell your children they could go to hell if they do not accept your view of the Gospel; that will scare them, and that is child abuse.

I believe we are living in such unique times, last days – maybe, but definitely times when we are strongly tempted to buy and sell our faith for acceptance in society. We will not be offensive and talk of hell, sin, or the need for an atonement. We don't want to offend someone, and in fact, we may be using hate speech in sharing the Gospel, and for that, we would be guilty of a criminal offense that would send us to prison. With that threat, you may be tempted to water down the Gospel and say that it doesn't matter what you believe, God is love, he will understand, so go ahead and have that abortion so you can enjoy life, go ahead and get drunk or curse if it will make you feel good after all God wants you to be happy.

For myself, I believe in a heaven and hell, I believe in Jesus who is the Son of God who died and rose from the dead and that He is the atonement for our sins and we are all sinners and must receive God's gift of salvation which is through Jesus Christ alone lest we go to hell when we die. If social media shuts me down for declaring that, accusing me of hate speech for saying they are going to hell without accepting Jesus as their Savior, then they can just take one flying leap, and when they land, they will receive a very warm (hot) welcome.

BELIEVE – HAYMAN

Acts 16:30-31: *"And brought them out, and said, Sirs, what must I do to be saved? And they said, Believe on the Lord Jesus Christ, and thou shalt be saved, and thy house."*

I have always wondered about this passage as it is a favorite salvation passage. The jailor fell to his knees before Paul and Silas and asked what must I do to be saved, and they replied, believe on the Lord Jesus Christ, and you will be saved. There is not a word in that little evangelistic scene about admitting you are a sinner and repenting.

I mean, what about *James 2:19: "Thou believest that there is one God; thou doest well: the devils also believe, and tremble."* James goes on to say in verse 20: "But wilt thou know, O vain man, that faith without works is dead?"

The word faith and belief in all these passages in the Greek are the same word, which is from the same root *pistis*, which is a legal term meaning to entrust, place something in the hands of another in confidence and trust that it is well taken care of. It would seem that this guard was pleading for his life when he asked what he must do to be saved. The word saved in Greek is *sozo* which means to seek divine safety. As a Roman guard over prisoners, he would forfeit his life if a prisoner escaped, but not only his life but his family's life as well. I doubt he was pleading for his soul salvation at this point.

In fact, the Aramaic makes it much clearer. The word for being saved is *'acha,'* which means to be spared your life in a physical sense, not a spiritual sense. What the jailor was asking Paul was, "What must I do to live and not be put to death by the Romans for failure in my duty." Paul's response was, "Trust in the Lord Jesus Christ." Here is the key to the whole thing. In

Aramaic, it is to trust in **our** Savior, the Messiah. This is a Gentile, and Paul is a Jew, but he is including this Gentile in the work of the Messiah, saying that this Jewish Messiah is also your Messiah – our Messiah. Grammatically in the Aramaic that we meant all who were present in the conversation. It was not an exclusive "our" as in the Jewish Messiah.

I believe this is where the process of salvation begins with this guard. He had to first trust in a Jewish Messiah and then accept Him as his God. To make Him *his*. His own personal God, a God that he will worship and learn to love. So, what about repentance? There is not a word about repentance. Is that not a part of salvation?

What is repentance? It is turning away from something and moving in another direction. For this Gentile, he knew to make the Messiah, Jesus Christ, his own personal God, he would have to turn away and forsake all other gods. He would have to make a commitment to this new God. That commitment meant putting his life and his family's life, which would not be worth a shekel if any prisoners escaped, into the hands of this Messiah God. He heard Paul and Silas singing hymns and witnessing to the other prisoners. He got the full Gospel message. He knew about repentance, but to put his life and the life of his family into the hands of this Messiah God and trust him to protect their lives, repentance would follow. It would easily be a part of the whole package.

Paul did not have to say repent. This was a desperate man, and if saying a sinner's prayer would get him off the hook, he was ready to do that. He even said, "What must I do." The word believe in Aramaic is *hayman*. This is also a legal word that means to give a loan in trust or to admit as evidence. It is also a word for confiding in someone. The guard would recognize that what Paul was saying was to give your life that you are afraid of losing and put it in trust to the Messiah.

You see, Paul went to the very root and heart of the salvation experience. One can pray a sinner's prayer but not really mean it in his heart. One can say he is entrusting his life to Jesus but not really mean it in his heart. But here was a desperate man who knew his life was on the line, and he knew if this Messiah God was to spare his life, he would have to be in good stead with Him. He would have known from Paul's witness to the other prisoners that this Messiah died for their sins and rose again and was alive. This old boy was already repenting. All he had to do was tell this Messiah God, Jesus, someone he could not see but believe, that He did exist and that his life now belonged to Him.

There was another time when a Pharisee was praying to God and bragged on all his good works, and next to him was a publican who said, "Lord be merciful to me a sinner." Luke 18:13. Jesus said this publican was justified or *dikaioo* in Greek, which is another legal term meaning to be right or declared innocent, as does the Aramaic word used in this verse *masadaq*. Jesus said nothing about believing in this situation. The very fact of his repentance to an unseen God justified him. He didn't even pray in Jesus' name, nor did he acknowledge Jesus. But in his heart, if he knew there was a Messiah who would die for his sins, he was ready to believe in Him. This guard acknowledged Jesus and the Messiah, the Son of God; he clearly was in a state of repentance, so all he had to do was *hayman*, give his life over to Jesus.

Here is something interesting, the word *hayma*n for entrusting or believing is also the word for hymns. A hymn is a song of dedication and surrender of your life, entrusting your life into the hands of Jesus. Every time you sing a hymn, you are confirming your commitment to believing on the Lord Jesus Christ for your salvation.

73
JOYFUL MESSAGE – TSEVA

Matthew 16:24: *"Then said Jesus unto his disciples, If any man will come after me, let him deny himself, and take up his cross, and follow me."*

Do you ever feel like you wasted your life? I suppose we all do at some time or another. I usually feel this way around the time of Founder's Week at Moody Bible Institute, where I graduated. Founder's Week is a time for alumni to gather together for a week of spiritual fellowship and uplift. I never attended. I am too ashamed to meet my former and successful classmates and have to face these now church leaders, founders of great Christian organizations and ministries, senior pastors of large and successful ministries or directors of mission boards, and when asked what I do, I have to say I drive a disability bus. I can almost feel the pat on the back from my former classmates, now successful and distinguished leaders in ministry, education, and Christian service, as they say; "Why that's alright Chaim, we knew you were never going to amount to anything, we knew you would never have any type of ministry or even a ministry at all. We figured you for someone who would end up driving a bus unable to afford retirement. But that's alright God uses people like you too."

Forty-five years I have studied the Word of God a minimum of three to four hours a day in the original languages. It seemed like every attempt I made throughout my life to start a ministry usually ended up in failure. I would pray and fast for my little ministry only to watch it go down in flames. I worked so hard for Jesus, sacrificing so much in my life. I felt God should reward me with at least a small church to preach from every week. All I asked for was just maybe twenty people, enough to afford a church building

Aramaic Word Study

and reasonable salary - never happened. He could at least allow me to have a full-time ministry so I did not have to work a full-time job. Never happened. Even when I taught in a Bible College, I needed to work a secular job just to make ends meet, and now at the age of 70 with a BA, MA, Ph.D. I still have to work a full-time low-level job driving a disability bus just to make ends meet and finance yet another noble attempt at a ministry that refuses to grow.

As I sit back and consider how many of my classmates from the Bible College and Seminary days have gone on to distinguished careers in ministry, gaining great fame in ministry, writing one book that outsells all the books I have written. I hear them on the radio or YouTube or a podcast preaching sermons that show no real depth of study in God's Words yet people will comment and just rave how wonderful these teachers are as I live in fear that I may one day meet one of these former classmates and be ashamed as I give an accounting of my life.

This morning as I was feeling sorry for myself, facing winter's harsh subzero weather and knowing I had to go out in it to drive my disability bus so I could pay my bills and support this ministry when others my age are enjoying retirement and could stay inside in a warm house if they so choose, God took me Matthew 16:24. "Ok, Ok, Lord, I know this pick up my cross business, I know I have to deny myself, etc., etc., etc., I think I have done a pretty good job of that over the last 70 years." But then God nudged me to look closely at the words "if any man will come after me." Some translations say, "wants to come after me." Yep, that is me in a nutshell; all my life, I have been trying to come after God or follow after God and look where it got me. I can hear your thoughts: "Oh, but don't you see, that is your problem; you are trying to do it rather than let God do it." Well, I've sat back for many years waiting for God to do it, that doesn't work either. I can hear others thinking: "But maybe your plans are not God's plans." I hate to admit it, but you are right.

Being adequately chastised, I felt prompted to study one word in the Aramaic from this verse. It is the word for want, which is *tseva* in Aramaic.

I searched this word out in the Midrash Rabbah, which is written in Aramaic, and found *tseva* is used for performing a service of bringing a message of hope and joy. Without modern communications in ancient times, messages were relayed by human messengers, and they often passed through great hardships to deliver a message. Yet, they fought hard for this position and service in hopes of being chosen to deliver a message of hope and joy. For it was worth all the trials and difficulties just to see the joy that message brought. This was really a coveted occupation to be a messenger, and only the most honored messengers were chosen to deliver the good news (Good News).

In more modern times, at the turn of the 20th century, Western Union delivered important and urgent messages. I read where Western Union delivery services paid very little to a messenger who depended upon tips to make an adequate wage. These messengers had ways to find out if the message they were to deliver was good news or bad news. If it was good news, they would encourage the receiver to read the message before receiving their tip, as the tip would often be larger if it was good news. If it was good news, the messenger would often hang around for a moment or two just to savor the joy of having brought the good news.

In Roman times the condemned were expected to carry the cross they were to die upon. It was a burdensome, humiliating, and disgraceful task facing mockery and shame from the crowds. Yet, it is the cross itself that carries the Good News. To carry the cross is doing just what is required of us in the Scriptures, letting it produce whatever shame, disgrace, or pain it may bring just for a *tseva* a joy in being able to deliver Good News.

74
LET THIS CUP PASS FROM ME

Matthew 26:39: *"And he went a little further, and fell on his face, and prayed, saying, O my Father, if it be possible, let this cup pass fro m me: nevertheless not as I will, but as thou wilt."*

We are now approaching the Easter holiday weekend, and I am constrained to offer a study that relates to Good Friday. For me, one of the great mysteries of this story is when Jesus was praying in the garden, and He was asking that the cup would pass him by. I have always been troubled by this passage of Scripture. Just what is the *cup*? I had been taught, even as a child, that this was the greatest lesson in obedience. Here Jesus is facing torture and death and is struggling against the will of his Father, not wanting to give up his life, but in the end, he submits and voluntarily gives up to the torture and death that awaits him, saying: *"Not my will but thine be done."*

The other day in my disability bus, I drove by the Olive–Harvey City College in Chicago. I asked my passenger who Olive–Harvey was. I was told that this college is really two colleges that merged, and both were named after two Vietnam soldiers who won the Medal of Honor. Both died in action. Benton Harvey, Jr. died when he charged a machine gun position to allow his comrades to carry two wounded soldiers into a helicopter, and PFC Milton Lee Olive died when he threw himself on a grenade to save his comrades. Both knew exactly what they were doing, and they did not hesitate to save the lives of their comrades, knowing full well it would cost them their own lives.

If human beings are capable of such heroic acts, then how much more is the God who created them capable of? Which begs the question, if God is perfect in love and loves us with this perfect love, why did He hesitate to go to the cross as this passage suggests? Did He really have this time of indecision, worried about His own gizzard? Then finally, after a long struggle, give up and say: "Alright, already, Father, you win, I'll go, I'll go if you order me." Ok, maybe you read this differently, maybe this passage does not trouble you, but it does me. I spent 40 years of my life studying Greek, Hebrew, and Aramaic so I could come to some peace over passages such as this one. So, you will have to forgive me if I happen to read my own bias into this passage.

Jesus spoke an Old Galilean form of Aramaic (not Greek) which scholars are just beginning to understand. When read from the Aramaic version of the Bible, the Peshitta, I come up with a little different rendering. First and foremost is the use of the word that is used for *cup* in Aramaic, which is the word *kasa*. It is identical to the Hebrew word *kavas*, which is also the word found in other Semitic languages used for a *stork*. The stork was noted for its tender loving care of its young. Legend has it that if one of the stork's chicks died, the mother stork would resurrect its young with its own blood. This is the same word Jesus used at the last supper when He said that *this cup* (not this wine) *is my blood*. In other words, this *nurturing love* is my blood. The Semitic mindset of the disciples would have allowed them to see a little play on words in this context. It would be his blood that would resurrect us and restore us to a rightful position with God.

In the garden, Jesus is praying that this *kasa (cup, nurturing love)* would pass from Him. In Greek, the word *pass* is *parelthato*, which means to *avert, avoid, or pass over*. But if this word for *pass* was spoken in Aramaic and later translated into Greek, it is possible the Aramaic might be closer to what Jesus said, which was *avar*. Now *avar* in Aramaic is the same word in Hebrew which has a wide range of meanings. The word itself is the picture of a river overflowing onto its banks. You could say that it is *passing over*, but more correctly, it would be *overwhelming*. Yes, the human part of Jesus was not looking forward to the coming torture and pain, but Jesus was not praying to get out of this situation but that *this cup,* or this *nurturing, sacrificial love* would *overwhelm* his physical body so it would not dread the coming pain.

Note in verse 37 it says he became *sorrowful*. The word *sorrowful* in the Aramaic is *kamar,* which means to burn or kindle and is used for a *burning love or compassion*. As Jesus was about to make the sacrifice of His own life, his entire being was filled with a burning love and compassion for mankind such that he says: "If it is possible let this *cup* or *this nurturing love avar overwhelm* me." The words, *if possible*, in Aramaic is *shekev* which literally means *if this happens*. In other words, Jesus is saying that if this is to happen tonight, then let this burning love, this nurturing love for mankind, just overwhelm me so that all I will think about is this consuming fire of love that I have. Just as Olive and Harvey thought only of their love for their buddies when they faced their final moments, it was that love that helped them to endure the agony of those moments. It was also that sacrificial love that Jesus had for each one of us that helped Him endure such horrendous pain and torture.

I don't believe Jesus sweat drops of blood over the fear of his impending torture and death, nor do I believe that the pressure of taking on our sins caused Him to sweat drops of blood, what I do believe is that He saw and knew at that moment the tremendous agony, pain, and suffering of mankind, He was so filled with love for each one of us that he could not endure the knowledge of what *our* pain and suffering were like. As God, he could not understand human suffering until he took on human flesh. Just like a mother prays that the suffering and pain of her child could somehow be removed from that child and placed upon her so that she would suffer rather than her child, so too our Heavenly Parent, Jesus, at that moment understood our suffering and pain and knew He could take it on. It was that knowledge and understanding of what sin had done to us and His empathy for our suffering that caused Him to suffer drops of blood. Being sinless, Jesus could not understand the torment of sin. In that moment, by taking on the sin of the world, Jesus understood what the torment of guilt was really like.

MERCY - YOD

John 8:4-6: *"They say unto him, Master, this woman was taken in adultery, in the very act. Now Moses in the law commanded us, that such should be stoned: but what sayest thou? This they said, tempting him, that they might have to accuse him. But Jesus stooped down, and with [his] finger wrote on the ground, [as though he heard them not]."*

Note: That last part in brackets, *as though he heard them not,* is not in the original inspired text.

Yesterday I was reading in the Talmud in Sanhedrin 2a-b. As I read, I once again wondered how Christians remain so aloof to the teachings of the ancient rabbis and sages and formulate their own opinions on difficult passages when it is not difficult if you give some attention to the ancient Jewish culture. This is one of many examples. Christians seem to just teach what some other teacher had taught who learned it from another teacher, but few ever really step out of their box and go to a Jewish source for answers. After 2,000 years, we Christians still ponder over passages that were easily understood by the Jewish people in the first century.

I have heard many Christians try to explain this passage in John 8:1-11 in ways that left me with many questions. What did Jesus write in the ground? How were they testing Jesus by quoting the Torah and saying the woman should be stoned? Why did these so call blood-thirsty Pharisees who were apparently very anxious to put this woman to death suddenly find they had to walk away when Jesus said: "He who is without sin, let him cast the first stone." Finally, what did the woman mean no one was accusing her? She was caught red-handed; why would someone not accuse her and stone her according to the law?

I have heard dozens of explanations of what Jesus wrote in the ground. One is that Jesus wrote the names of the men who committed adultery with this woman. This seems to be very popular because: "Ha Ha, Jesus really caught them red-handed." What Jesus really did, however, was much cleverer and more profound than that.

Around 300 AD, Constantine conquered all of Europe and wanted to consolidate his kingdom. To do this, he needed to have a unified religion. Thus, he began to universalize Christianity with other pagan religions, bringing in pagan worship practices. The Jewish Christians rebelled. Well, rebellion was one thing Constantine would not tolerate, so he threw all the Jews out of the church, including their two thousand years of culture, traditions, and Jewish writings. The church then declared the Jews were Christ-killers, and that became the orthodox teaching passing into Protestantism with Martin Luther, who took a dim view of the Jews. It was not until 1962 when Pope John attended a mass where the priest was performing his obligatory Good Friday sermon condemning the Jews as Christ-killers. The pope was aghast that the church still clung to this dogma. He declared the Jews were not Christ-killers and the priests were never again to preach a sermon against the Jews.

You see, Pope John was a scholar who studied the Talmud, and I believe he read what I read in Sanhedrin 2a-b and realized that the Jews as a whole in the first century were anything but Christ-killers. Oh, to be sure, there was a small segment of Jews who wanted to put Jesus to death, but it was a very small segment. Let me quote to you from the Talmud something that was in practice during the day of Jesus:

"Monetary matters are decided by a court of three judges . . . capital crimes {like adultery} by a tribunal of twenty-three judges. . . . From where is this derived? For it is written in Numbers 35:24-25: "The community shall judge . . . and the community shall save"—we need a community of judges arguing to convict the accused, and a community of judges arguing to exonerate him. Thus, we have twenty a "community" indicating a minimum of 10, as per Numbers 14:27, conviction requires a majority of two as per Exodus 23:2, and a court of law cannot have an even number of judges; thus, we need twenty-three judges (22 so that there should be a majority of 2 over the 10 "saving" judges, and another judge so that the court should not be even-numbered)." Sanhedrin 2 a-b.

Twenty-three judges were necessary for a conviction of a capital crime like adultery. These Pharisees who took this woman to Jesus knew the law very well and knew Jesus could not condemn this woman under present Jewish law, for you needed a court of 23 judges. Aside from this were many other hoops, such as the nature of the witnesses and their testimonies to jump through so that by the first century, the Jews made it virtually impossible to execute anyone. That is why Jesus had to be tried before Pilate. By the time the Jews returned from their captivity, they could no longer stomach the idea of killing someone even if he was a criminal. So, they, as we have done in our country, created so many checks and balances, appeals, and rules of law that it would take years for a person to be executed if he is executed at all.

These Pharisees were not trying to kill this woman; they were trying to put Jesus in a tight situation where He had to admit that the oral law, the Traditions of the Fathers, carried as much weight as the Torah. You see, they believed that whatever was bound on earth by two or three in agreement would be bound in heaven. The Talmud teaches that where two or three are gathered together in agreement, the Divine presence is in their midst. In other words, where two or three are in agreement that watching a football game on Sunday is in violation of the Sabbath law of keeping the day holy, then they would bind this on earth, and it would therefore be bound in heaven. Hence the authority of the Tradition of the Fathers or the Talmud.

But Jesus was teaching against the authority of the Tradition of the Fathers and many of the laws of the Tradition of the Fathers or the Talmud, so these Pharisees were testing Jesus, trying to back Him in a corner where He had to admit to the authority of the Tradition of the Father or appear as a heartless, vindictive teacher totally out of character with the true nature of a loving God.

However, Jesus did them one better. I asked a rabbi what he thought Jesus wrote in the ground, and he laughed. "Must I, a Jew, explain your own New Testament to you? Jesus obviously wrote a Yod for the name of God, the feminine form, the loving, benevolent, caring nature of God. The Yod has the same significance in Aramaic as in Hebrew, so the Pharisees clearly knew what Jesus was saying or writing. He could not speak that name nor write it, but he could write the Yod and the Pharisees knew what He meant. Jesus appealed to the mercy side of God, the side that forgives. Had he wrote an

Aleph for Elohim, it would show the masculine side, the disciplinary side that would condemn the woman. Instead, Jesus simply told the Pharisees, we all deserve to die for our sins; if there is anyone of you who is sinless and does not need the mercy of God, let him cast the first stone. Of course, they all had to leave, for they knew they needed God's mercy as much as this poor woman."

I don't know about you, but I think it is time we begin to study some of the teachings of the founders of our Christian faith, the Jews, and perhaps it is now time that we begin to see the fulfillment of Zechariah 8:23: *Thus saith the LORD of hosts; In those days [it shall come to pass], that ten men shall take hold out of all languages of the nations, even shall take hold of the skirt of him that is a Jew, saying, We will go with you: for we have heard [that] God [is] with you.*

About the Author

Chaim Bentorah is the pseudonym of a Gentile Christian who taught college-level Biblical Hebrew and is an Amazon Bestselling Author. He prepared his students to take the placement exams for graduate school. He has now developed a method of study where he can prepare any Believer, regardless of age or academic background, to study the Word of God using Biblical Hebrew.

Chaim Bentorah received his B.A. degree from Moody Bible Institute in Jewish Studies and his M.A. degree from Denver Seminary in Old Testament and Hebrew and his PhD in Biblical Archeology. His Doctoral Dissertation was on the "Esoteric Structure of the Hebrew Alphabet." He has taught Classical Hebrew at World Harvest Bible College for thirteen years and also taught Hebrew for three years as a language course for Christian Center High School. He is presently teaching Biblical Hebrew and Greek to pastors in the Metro Chicago area.

www.chaimbentorah.com

Other books by Chaim Bentorah

- Stargates, Time Travel, And Alternate Universes
- Time Loop: Seeing America's Future in Persia's Past
- Ten Words That Will Change Everything You Know About God
- Does The Bible Really Sat That?
- Treasures of the Deep
- Learning God's Love Language
- Learning God's Love Language Workbook
- Hebrew Word Study: Revealing The Heart Of God
- Journey into Silence
- Whom My Soul Loves
- Intimacy With God
- Is This Really Revival?
- Biblical Truths From Uncle Otto's Farm

Learn Hebrew Word Study from Chaim Bentorah!
Special introductory offer (Just $0.99 your first month!)

Do you want to go further in your Hebrew word study?
Join Chaim Bentorah's HebrewWordStudy.com

Just imagine, having all this at your fingertips, on demand!

- More than 1000 Hebrew studies: $249.00 value
- Hebrew Alphabet poster (download): $10 value.
- 8-hour video Hebrew Word Study Course: $50 value
- 9 Chaim Bentorah e-books free! $90 Value
- Learning God's Love Language audio: $24.99 value
- Weekly live-stream teaching: $499 value
- 24/7 access: "Ask Chaim": $199 value
- Video Hebrew word studies: $499 value
- Hebrew Alphabet video teaching: $50 Value
- 20% off insider discount on Chaim Bentorah books.
- and much more – this just keeps growing!

Visit www.ChaimBentorah.com

Printed in France by Amazon
Brétigny-sur-Orge, FR